W9-BXV-478

Passed Thru Fire is not a good book; it is a great book. A must-read if you have any connections to boys or men.

DR. DAVID OLSHINE
Director of Youth Ministries
Columbia International University
Columbia, SC

Thank God somebody is doing some clear thinking and writing about how to help boys become real men. I'll be recommending *Passed Thru Fire* to every parent whose home has been blessed with boys.

WAYNE RICE
Director of Understanding Your Teenager

If you want to challenge a generation of young men to live an adventure-filled life in reckless abandon to the call of the gospel, *Passed Thru Fire* is for you.

REV. RICH VAN PELT
National Director of Ministry Relationships
Compassion International
Colorado Springs, CO

The boys and men about whom Rick Bundschuh writes are gritty, unruly, energetic, and disruptive. So also is his book! But then boys want to be men, but don't know how. This book shows them.

D. STUART BRISCOE
Minister-at-Large
Elmbrook Church
Brookfield, WI

Passed Thru Fire clearly maps the challenges we face and gives positive solutions for how we can bring our boys into a God-centered adulthood.

JOHN RUHLMAN
Founder and Lead Pastor
Life Church
Temecula, CA

Rick lives and writes with a contagious passion for men, particularly about the journey to manhood every boy faces.

CRAIG McCONNELL
Pastor
Imago Dei Fellowship
Colorado Springs, CO

I have learned the importance of reaching, and sometimes reclaiming, the "young lions" of the teenage community. It's great to read a book that puts these vital issues into perspective!

KEN McCOY
JumpStart Ministries
Escondido, California

PASSED THRU FIRE

RICK BUNDSCHUH

Tyndale House Publishers, Inc.
Wheaton, Illinois

Visit Tyndale's exciting Web site at www.tyndale.com

Copyright © 2003 by Rick Bundschuh. All rights reserved.

Cover photograph of climber copyright © 2003 by IT International ltd./eStock Photo.
All rights reserved.

Author photo taken by John Russell. All rights reserved.

Edited by Lisa A. Jackson

Designed by Luke Daab

Unless otherwise indicated, all Scripture quotations are taken from the *Holy Bible,* New International Version®. NIV®. Copyright © 1973, 1978, 1984 by International Bible Society. Used by permission of Zondervan Publishing House. All rights reserved.

Scripture quotations marked TLB are taken from *The Living Bible,* copyright © 1971.
Used by permission of Tyndale House Publishers, Inc., Wheaton, Illinois 60189.
All rights reserved.

Some Scripture taken from *THE MESSAGE.* Copyright © 1993, 1994, 1995, 1996, 2000, 2001, 2002. Used by permission of NavPress Publishing Group.

Library of Congress Cataloging-in-Publication Data

Bundschuh, Rick, date.
Passed thru fire : bringing boys into meaningful manhood / Rick Bundschuh.
p. cm.
Includes bibliographical references.
ISBN 0-8423-7634-8 (sc)
1. Church work with youth. 2. Boys—Religious life. I. Title.
BV4450 .B86 2003
259′.22—dc21 2002155560

Printed in the United States of America

08 07 06 05 04 03
6 5 4 3 2 1

For Mason, Justin, and Hudson.
May you be men of wild adventure, wisdom, and grace.

Table of Contents

Acknowledgments

I owe the real debt of gratitude for the vast amount of ideas in this book to my mentor, father figure, and friend E. G. Von. This man not only took the role abdicated by my real father and guided me through the rough seas of adolescence, but he has also impressed on me true and treasured wisdom about the workings of the world and, in particular, the world of men.

I'm sure E. G. would have written this book long ago if he weren't busy doing more important things, like washing the lice out of little kids' hair—only part of his ministry to the poor just across our borders.

I am also deeply indebted to the team at Tyndale for being willing to take risk on this project, and to Dale Reeves and Paul Learned at Standard Publishing for publishing my resources to help boys pass through fire.

I also greatly appreciate the support of the guys in my Kauai Christian Fellowship men's group—Colin, Scott, Del, and Jimbo—who sat through the reading of many chapters and helped with their affirmation and ideas. I owe special thanks to my office manager, Monica, for her assistance with editing.

Gratitude of immense proportions goes to my beautiful wife, Lauren, who gave much encouragement and support for this project.

Foreword

I started writing this book in 1985 and tried to get a publisher interested.

No bites.

In addition to a collection of politely worded rejection letters, I received a few tidbits of advice that usually went something like this: "Rick, Christian books are sold primarily to women, so you have to realize how suicidal it would be for a publisher to come out with a book that might offend its biggest customers."

I could see their point. After all, the feminist movement was in overdrive at the time, and men were panic-stricken as they tried to sort out their roles or simply bury themselves in their caves until the storm blew over.

Since that time, extreme feminism has been relegated to the lunatic fringe or the college campus (which often are the same thing), and a few daring books directed at the dynamics of men, boys, and the church have escaped through the net.

Friends who knew that I was working on a book about the role of the church in the lives of boys and men made sure to drop off some recent books in the same genre. I found them to be insightful.

Robert Lewis tackled great issues in *Raising a Modern-Day Knight,* and John Eldredge fired up the souls of many men with his beautiful book *Wild at Heart.* Another jewel was Leon J. Podles's worthy—and, I fear, much underread—volume *The Church Impotent.*

With the exception of Mr. Podles's book, which I had read earlier, I made a conscious decision *not* to peruse any works by other authors commenting on similar issues until after I had finished the first, revised draft of this book.

There were several reasons for this. The first is that most writers are also readers. As a reader, it's very easy to pick up ideas, words, and thoughts from the works of others and store them away deep in some mental cranny. Sometimes these thoughts return to a writer's mind disguised as his or her own original musings.

While no author is immune to this, my hope has been to put down on paper thoughts, experiences, and observations that, as much as possible, have come from my own journey and the whispers of the Lord.

But there was a second reason why I waited to read these books. I wanted to see if other men shared my observations and my way of thinking as a Christian man . . . or if I was just out to lunch.

When I did finally read the other books, I was pleased to find not only parallel thinking but in some places identical values, concepts, and words. This encouraged the part of me that wants to sound more like a teacher than a loose cannon.

While the direction of this book might not sit well with some women readers (and some men!), it's not my desire to offend these wonderful and uniquely different creatures God has fashioned. Rather, it's my goal to give back to them the kind of men they have always wanted and knew could exist: men of honor, courage, integrity, loyalty, and deep spirituality, men who know how to love and also know how to lead.

Finally, this book may produce frustration. The problems I identify and the solutions I offer may resonate with you and produce a call to action, but may only be met with yawns by those in positions to make changes.

Prayer and prodding can help.

Bottom-up leadership can help too. Loan this book to a friend and discuss ideas that you think are timely. If he (or she) senses the same need for change, your yearnings may eventually turn into a tide. God often uses his sheep to awaken those who are in the role of shepherd.

Rick Bundschuh
Kauai, Hawaii

Introduction

An epiphany.

Crossing the Rubicon.

The Passage.

These are the words an adult might have used to describe what happened on that chilly and foggy fall morning. But for one lanky, sun-bleached, fourteen-year-old boy, it was simply the confirmation of that which he had been seeking: his manhood.

Bill Blankenship's dented and rust-tinged station wagon pulled up in the deserted beach parking lot at the crack of dawn. Bill, or "Coach Blankenship," as the ninth-grade boys wedged into his car respectfully called him, was a schoolteacher. He was really old in their minds, possibly even *forty*.

But Mr. Blankenship had something that none of the young teens who tumbled out of his car had. He had experience, he had wisdom, he had skill, and he had courage. In short, he had manhood.

Bill Blankenship was an athlete. In particular, he was a

waterman—a surfer, a diver, a sailor of the rough-and-tumble old school style where only the truly fit and brave could survive. He could read the ocean. He could understand the significance of weather charts and knew the likelihood of some distant storm in the South Pacific producing waves. He was strong, judicious, brave, and accomplished.

The boys rubbing the sleep out of their eyes were watermen wanna-bes. Young surfers. Kids whose verbal feats boasted of far more than their young years had actually experienced. In contrast to Bill, they were weak, foolish, cocky (yet secretly fearful), and completely inexperienced.

On this day, just after dawn, the boys and the man stood together on a rocky outcropping, peering into the foggy sea and listening to the thunderous crack of waves breaking a quarter mile offshore.

Every boy in the group had bragged about his prowess in the ocean. Each one had responded with boastful excitement when Mr. Blankenship offered to take them surfing at a place that would, in his words, "really make a man out of them." But none was prepared for the simple, elegant test that would become his rite of passage.

The boys stood huddled together as their teacher assessed the situation. "It's gonna be big!" he quietly breathed.

Big? What does that mean? was the unspoken thought racing through each young mind. *Big like a wall, big like a house, or big like an apartment building? How big is big?*

Most of these boys had only seen "big" on movies or from the safety of a beach. This surf was "big" and Mr. Blankenship was obviously planning to go out in it.

Blankenship casually walked to his station wagon and slipped off his sweatpants and jacket. His tanned, lean body had lost some of the suppleness of youth, but his fitness was still remarkable. He yanked a giant surfboard from the rack and began to rub wax on it (this would keep his feet from slipping).

None of the boys followed suit.

When he had finished waxing up his board, he turned toward the cluster of youngsters and, with a slight grin, said, "So, who's going to be man enough to join me?"

The line had been drawn, the glove thrown, the challenge made.

Not one boy on that fog-swirled point had an ounce of desire to paddle into the mist toward "big."

It was a deciding moment. Here, a man's man was inviting mere boys to step into his world. He was challenging their manhood, calling for them to lay down the cards they had boasted of holding.

And soon he would be able to separate the cowardly braggart from the genuine article. He could bear witness to their peers. He had the power to confirm or destroy any pretense of manhood they might attempt to pass off in the future.

No one spoke. One by one, the boys began to pull their wave craft off the station wagon's rack and nervously run the cold wax across the decks of their surfboards. Mr. Blankenship pursed his lips, nodded, then turned his back on the boys. He paused for a moment on a small sliver of barnacle-encrusted reef; then he leaped, board and all, into the chilly water.

The four young teenagers, including the shivering, skinny, blond boy, began to line up behind him. All but one. The last boy fiddled with his clothes, paced around, drummed up a sudden cough, and mumbled something about catching up with everyone later.

Everyone in the pack understood the boy's hesitation. Each of them had that same live nerve ending of fear pulsing through them. Each boy wrestled against the inviting idea of staying safe and warm on the beach rather than following a potential madman into unknown waters.

The boys who chose to follow Coach Blankenship out to sea early that morning had only just begun their initiation. The real test would come when they mustered the courage to paddle down the face of house-size swells and stand on their feet. Three teens, including the lanky, bleach-haired boy, entered the water and rode waves that day.

That morning, three boys entered manhood—and one stayed a child.

The four boys knew it. Their companions knew it. Coach Blankenship knew it. Soon the school would know it.

I know this story well because I was the lanky, bleach-haired boy.

I was fortunate enough to have had a rite of passage that, while dangerous, was within an acceptable range of risk. I was fortunate enough to have a decent and upright man validate and lead that experience (although I doubt that this was anything more to him than another surf trip with a bunch of green kids).

This pivotal point in my life was no doubt more by accident than design. Like most boys my age, I was grasping for some kind of official stamp acknowledging my manhood. I was looking for something that once and for all would separate me from being a fearful boy to being a courageous young man, affirmed by other men.

This was my opportunity, my moment to seize the prize. After all, I called myself a surfer. In the safety of the lunch court, I boasted about my big-wave prowess. That day, it was time to ante up.

It wasn't about foolishness. The waves were conquerable. It was about actually being the person I laid claim to be.

If I had joined my quivering comrade in sitting out the surf session in the warmth and safety of the car, I would have had to live down my shame and hope for another chance to take up the gauntlet of manhood (which is just what my buddy did on the next big-wave day).

Many of the boys I grew up with weren't so blessed. Many damaged themselves and did damage to the souls and bodies of others in their clumsy, groping attempts to find some kind of affirmation of their manhood.

Times have not changed.

Today, young teens still fumble about blindly trying to find that mystical line in the sand that separates boyhood from manhood.

I believe that God has provided an answer for them. I believe God has given us the standards by which a male can measure his manhood:

righteousness, integrity, courage, self-control, responsibility, and love and protection for the weak. I also believe God has provided powerful mentors to model God-centered manhood and guide boys toward it. The church can provide these mentors, and it must be the essential tool in moving our boys into manhood.

But there needs to be change. We in the Christian community must rethink what we do with the young males in our care and how we do it. The men of the church will have to get deeply involved in order for boys to become men through watching and emulating them.

The purpose of this book is to bring to light the needs of boys in our culture, particularly in the Christian church. The plan is also to give practical, sensible, and workable solutions that can be duplicated or can serve as models or starting points for the passage of our boys into manhood.

Left on their own, without help from godly men, these "uninitiated" boys often gravitate towards all that is the worst in the male world. They become aggressors rather than protectors, sexual conquerors rather than committed lovers, exploiters rather than givers. They are spiritually and emotionally closed rather than open, domineering rather than sharing, twisted and wicked rather than righteous and virtuous.

If they can't find a way to connect with a man's world, some boys become wounded—pliant pushovers who are unattractive to both women and men.

This book is a direct challenge to the church—a challenge to take seriously the role and responsibility we have to raise our boys into capable, strong, and confident men. It's a challenge to do something rather than merely discuss the fact that something should be done. It's a challenge to create an environment where God-centered manhood can be initiated, affirmed, and celebrated for the good of our generation and the ones to come.

We went through fire and water,
but you brought us to a place of abundance.

psalm 66:12

There comes a time in every rightly constructed boy's life when he has a raging desire to go somewhere and dig for hidden treasure.

—Mark Twain

1 THE BOYS' CLUB

We had a boys' club. Constructed of scrap wood, it was a glorified lean-to, held together with crooked nails. The interior was decorated with scavenged goods from the neighborhood, including three-legged chairs and a deeply stained sofa spewing old stuffing. Several dented clip-on lights, which were strung along a tangle of extension cords, lit the ramshackle retreat. The cramped floor was covered in mismatched patches of funky, used carpeting. Outside, ominous warning signs with crude skulls and crossbones were posted: *Girls Keep Out! Boys Only!*

We—the fledgling junior engineers—built and decorated the clubhouse ourselves and met inside to plan grand adventures and daring plots. While younger members kept a lookout for the enemy—girls or adults—senior members set the important agenda. It was different each day.

Sometimes we would prowl construction zones to find "slugs" (coin-shaped, metal electric-box punch outs) and then spend the rest of the day filing them down to match the size of a quarter in the hopes that we could con a soda machine out of its contents.

Other days would be spent on worthwhile endeavors such as digging up the backyard in an attempt to create a tunnel to the house next door; building a catapult that would fling mud or dried dog poop over a fence and (hopefully) onto the "enemy"; or designing a dry-land dogsled out of commandeered roller-skate wheels, plywood, and one unsuspecting dog. Then there were agendas that included exploring the mysteries of the water-drainage system or eliminating whole colonies of ants with a magnifying glass and then having burn battles by turning the beams onto each other.

One morning it was decided that Barbie dolls were actually secret agents and must therefore be executed for treason. Each boy with a sister was required to swipe a plastic Barbie so she could be lined up against the wall and sent to her maker (which I believe was Mattel) in a volley of BBs.

Wrestling, exploring, daring, boasting, building, destroying—we were boys!

We have since grown to be men and have boys of our own, but the memory of boyhood has never been forgotten.

I married a woman. She had no experience growing up as a boy. Therefore when our two oldest boys began to manifest a desire to pull the wings off flies, salt down snails, and fill their pockets with strange rocks, bolts, magnets and, on occasion, some very dead things, my wife, Lauren, started to panic. "Are they normal?" she asked.

It was then that I told her about the boys' club, the countless orphaned ants my childhood had created, flying poop, suddenly legless cockroaches, terrorized neighborhoods, making slugs into quarters, exploding the lids off bottles with vinegar and baking soda, and other exciting stories that took on a new glow as I relived them once again.

She slowly moved away from me as I was talking and finally said, "Are you saying they got this from you?"

"No . . . uh, well, maybe I gave them a couple of ideas, but they do this stuff because they're boys!" I stammered.

As I rolled the memories of the boys' club over in my mind, I realized that what we were actually doing, in a goofy, unknowing, clumsy sort of way, was practicing to be men.

We built things. Men build things.

We destroyed things. Men destroy things.

We dominated nature. Men dominate nature.

We created adventure. Men create adventure.

In these and many other areas, our play paralleled a reality that in a few years we would be called to live out.

No one told us to do these things; they were a part of our being. A divine stamp separated us from the feminine members of the human race. We were boys. We would be men . . . if we could find the way.

Finding the way is the most difficult and mysterious part. Somehow, we all were slowly becoming aware (despite the cardboard manhood we saw in movies) that *real* men are made, not born. We understood that anatomical adult maleness is not always the same as manhood and that in some vague way, we knew that other men had something to do with affirming and acknowledging manhood. But beyond that, the path to manhood swirled with the fog of uncertainty.

THE MAN'S LOT IN LIFE

Sometimes my wife says, "I should have been born a man."

Perhaps this comes from the fact that as a dentist, she's in an often male-dominated profession and thus feels out of place in some way. Or maybe it's her competitive spirit or utter disregard for spending the day shopping. I don't know. But I do know that I can't ever remember a time when the thought *I should have been born a woman* popped into my head.

As I came to manhood, I began to hear a number of outside voices suggesting that the world would be a better place if I (and all the other little male babies) had been born a woman.

Women, they explained, had been viciously held back by men, but if they were only allowed the chance, they would create a world that men had been unable to create—a world of peace, love, harmony, beauty, and unshaven armpits.

These women burned their bras to make their point. I was an incredulous witness to the flowering of the feminist movement.

While the most vocal and stringent wave of feminism is no longer active, a residue of its thinking clings to our culture and seeps into the psyches of both men and women.

For example, many trees have been wasted over the last few decades to create books that propose the idea that men are somehow generally to blame for the problems of the world and, in particular, the problems of women. The cult of female victimhood is still large and boisterous.

In some circles, it is seriously suggested that in our "enlightened" day and age, the aggressive nature of males is a primitive leftover and our society would be a kinder, gentler place if it became matriarchal in design and government.

Men are still seen as forming boys' clubs with "Keep Out" signs created in clever ways. Power, money, and influence are, according to these theories, said to be held tightly by male hands. We males are the Illuminati, the Mafioso, and all things malicious.

On the surface it seems obvious that men really do control power, money, and influence. But that idea is, as we shall see, a bit simplistic and one-sided.

While men have no doubt been coconspirators to the various miseries visited upon the world, it's shortsighted and unfair to suggest that somehow men have it better or easier, or that they profit more than women by fortune of their gender.

Now, in some ways, the lot of men is better (especially if what you enjoy doing takes a strong body), but in other ways the lot of men is considerably worse and much less powerful than that of the opposite sex. For example:

Men often pay for being men with their lives. In a time of war, it's primarily men who find themselves in harm's way—not as "collateral damage," but as intentional targets. Even in countries like the Soviet Union or Israel that actively promote an equal opportunity for women to serve in frontline forces, the fact is that very few women find their way into combat situations.[1]

In the United States, the selective service requires *only* boys to register with the draft board at eighteen, and if a draft is activated, it selects *only* males. In the event of war, the jobs that call for a life to be sacrificed will almost universally be required from the male.

Giving your life for the protection of your country is the unequal opportunity that even some of the most hardened feminists wouldn't wish to rectify, especially if it required the lives of their own daughters.

Any young man who has opened a world history book knows that in the last hundred years, millions of boys like him have donned a uniform, marched to war, and never returned. And he knows that he could very well join that number.

Men know that they may have to pay with life or limb as part of the duty *required* by their gender.

Men pay in the workplace as well. Find a job that is dangerous, potentially fatal, or hazardous to your health, and you will find that it's almost without exception dominated by men.[2]

Although not a Christian, Dr. Warren Farrell writes of the dangers inherent in being a male in his book *The Myth of Male Power.* He points out that "94 percent of occupational deaths occur to men" and "every workday hour, one construction worker in the United States loses his life."[3]

[1] Martin Van Creveld, "Why Israel Doesn't Send Women into Combat," *Parameters,* Spring 1993: 5-9. Also, Marlene Cimons, "Women in Combat: Panama Stirs Debate," *The Los Angeles Times*, 11 January 1990.

[2] During a one-year study (1992-93), job-related fatalities for men were 17,683 and for women, 1,453. Source: Census of Fatal Occupational Injuries, Andrew Knestaut, Bureau of Labor Statistics.

[3] Warren Farrell, *The Myth of Male Power* (New York: Simon & Shuster, 1993), 106.

Of course, we probably don't need Dr. Farrell to document this for us. All we have to do is consider those hundreds who bravely rushed into, not out of, the World Trade Center on September 11 and gave their lives in the process.

They were *all* men.[4]

Men pay with their lifespan. They tend to live shorter lives than women; ironically, this is particularly true in countries that are highly industrialized.

Disease (often stress related), suicide, and accidents deplete men's ranks considerably faster than they do women's.

When we have needed a guinea pig for medical purposes or someone to be a test pilot, the candidates have usually been male.

Men also pay in the courtroom. Men are far more likely to lose their families if they end up getting a divorce. Although the eyes of lady justice are blindfolded, she usually responds more favorably to a woman's voice. There is a clear judicial bias against the husband in a divorce case. It's tougher for a man to gain primary parental custody based on his ability to care for the child in an equal or better manner than his former spouse. He must *prove* he has the ability to nurture better or equal to his former spouse; she is awarded with the *presumption* of ability to nurture on the basis of her gender.

Today, courts across the nation are being asked to make decisions on the appropriateness of child support payments for children that, after DNA testing, turn out *not* to be the actual biological offspring of the "father." While the actual father of the child is carrying none of the financial weight, judges often force these former husbands or faked-out fathers to continue to make their child-support payments, refusing to force the woman to make restitution for monies fraudulently received.

If a man and a woman commit a crime together, statistics show that the man will almost always "take the drop" and get a harsher sentence than the woman.

[4] You can see a photo of each of these men at this moving Web site: www.nytimes.com/library/national/091101rescuers.html

Men pay in the courtroom of public opinion. When a male politician becomes morally compromised and is discovered with a mistress or becomes embroiled in an affair, he could lose his office or have his career stained for life. The mistress or other woman in the affair may appear on talk shows, become a celebrity, make the cover (and centerfolds) of magazines, and earn millions on book deals, usually without condemnation. Both are guilty. One pays, one profits.

When the late, celebrated Princess Diana had an affair, public opinion became sympathetic towards her, agonizing for her apparent loneliness. When Prince Charles had an affair, he was labeled a rat.

Men in today's culture also must deal with a vast array of confusing relationship issues. They understand the traditional role of men but also hear voices that tell them to move away from that "caveman ethic" and become a new, remodeled version of a man: one with strength and sensitivity, a soul of steel that oozes with emotion. Many men struggle to understand their proper role. For example, most men would never consider the possibility of dropping their career to stay home and raise the kids while their wife worked, even if they wanted to. But they know many "career" women who have chosen just that. Therefore, because many men feel they have no option but to work for their families, while women may decide to quit and become stay-at-home parents at will, they often struggle to take "career" women seriously. Men think of themselves as lifers in the workplace and of most women as visitors who may choose, or would choose, if they had the chance, to opt out to raise a family at any time.

Women, on the other hand, very often choose a life partner based at least partly on his security factor—his ability to provide as many positive options as possible. You can see this at work in everyday conversations.

If a male tells his friends that he has met "Miss Right," the first question from guys is often "What does she look like?" When a female meets "Mr. Right," the question sometimes becomes "What does he do?" And if what he does is flip burgers, write sonnets, or make pottery, the next comment might be "Well, I'm sure he is a nice guy, but I think you could do better." The not-so-subtle implication is that a man's virility is judged by the weight of his wallet.

When choosing a mate, men rarely factor in a woman's ability to provide fiscal security. They *assume* the role of supplier.

Regardless of noise to the contrary, men get this signal loud and clear. They know that what most women really want is a man who can provide them with security and options. And one of those options women hope for is to be taken care of while they raise the children.

Men are often faced with frustrating mixed messages. If a wife says she's disappointed they can't afford a bigger house, nicer car, or the latest decor in *Better Homes and Gardens,* her husband feels he's not providing for his family. But in order to make the money for these things, he must work harder and longer. If the man chooses to take on the extra work or the advancement that pays more but requires more hours, he's criticized for spending all his time at work instead of with the family. If he chooses not to take the extra work, he feels as if he's not truly providing for his family. Either way, he fails.

The church in most modern societies rarely celebrates simplistic living and godly contentment (1 Timothy 6:6), and it leaves men struggling to meet the fiscal and emotional expectations of women in a way doomed to end in dissatisfaction.

Most men are aware of their lot in life. Most don't complain all that much about it. They accept it and often embrace it. Ever since God required Adam to work the land by the sweat of his brow, there's been a tactical understanding among men: Ours is a uniquely different calling from that of the other gender. We are different from women.

- Men love in a different way than women.
- Men dream in a different way than women.
- Men work out their relationships in a different way than women.
- Men react to danger and competition in a different way than women.

- Men respond emotionally in a different way than women.
- Men grow spiritually in a different way than women.

This is what boys are rehearsing and toughening each other up for. Boys are men in the making. Males now, but men someday. At least that's the goal.

In our culture, most boys grope their way into manhood, stumbling and fumbling along the way. A good majority make it. Some don't. These remnants are adult males but not men; they grow old but don't grow up. Men do not respect them as men.

Some boy-men disappear into a bottle or a chemical blur.

Some boy-men attempt to stay in a hedonistic Peter Pan state where lack of responsibility, uncommitted sexuality, and immaturity are the hallmarks.

Some boy-men become empty-souled toy collectors, adding things to their garages while avoiding things of eternal substance and meaning.

Some boy-men evaporate into a mere mob. They go with whatever is vogue among male rabble. They become intoxicated voyeurs who feed upon the excitement and life of others as they themselves sink into the comfortable seat of passivity.

Some boy-men feign manhood by building a facade of rebellion, trying to pass off true masculinity with a "me against the world" lifestyle that's hostile and noncommunicative, antisocial and violent. Hollywood's offerings of *Dirty Harry, Rambo,* and *Die Hard* nurture and feed on this inadequate definition of maleness.

Men, do you remember what it was like to be a boy? With a small bit of dredging, each of us can remember some vital point of contact with the world of men that we aspired to.

Not only do we remember; we feel, believe it or not.

We feel what women can't feel.

If you're a male, do you remember what it was like to feel the sting of this one word, usually spat out rather than said?

Sissy!

One word. Not much of a word either. It just implies that you're a sister rather than a brother.

But for a boy, that word goes straight to the hot nerve ending in his soul.

A reaction will be immediate, almost an impulse. *Wham!* That little word, often married to a few other similar words—*wussy, wimp, chicken*—goes to the gut of a boy and produces results. A clenched fist swinging through the air, a verbal exchange of similar taunts, adamant denials or, in the case of one already pressed down, further compression and the frantic feeling a trapped animal must know.

The feeling of having our bravery challenged, our power impugned, or our manhood derided is dramatic and potent for men. Those feelings create strong reactions in the soul of a wanna-be boy as well as any man.

BOYS NATURALLY TILT TOWARD EXTREMES

The less comfortable you are with your position, especially in the eyes of those who matter, the greater the extreme you'll swing toward in order to prove yourself to others.

The macho male strut, the womanizing bravado, and the ultra-extreme trappings exhibited by some are rarely typical of those males who hold true power and prestige in the world of men. Those actions *are* typical of those who are trying to prove a manhood they aren't sure of.

At a particular time in a boy's journey, the extremes begin to take hold.

A boy may suddenly refuse to walk down the Barbie aisle in the toy store. He won't touch anything pink. Ponies are out; stallions are in. The smiling and gentle *Thomas the Tank Engine* gives way to fierce-faced monster trucks. Many boys become fascinated by gore, speed, flames, and power.

At this point, boys start to identify with whatever is the strongest representation of manhood presented by the culture at the time. Wrestlers, sports figures, action-movie heroes, and martial arts fighters become the coin of the boy realm. And they don't have to be real; they only need be representative.

As a boy seeks out the strongest, most undeniable male image available, he'll begin to demean softer values. A sweaty, rough, massive, gritty, macho (and practically unattainable) manhood is hoisted to a place of honor, while ethics, compassion, tenderness, sensitivity, care—all those attributes that seem to the boy to be in the realm of the feminine—are ignored, if not despised.

In this rush toward the extreme, a boy will often sweep aside the church, which has never been particularly comfortable expressing the masculinity of our Lord or dwelling on the muscular side of our faith. With its sweetness and often light message, the church doesn't fit inside the parameters of manhood to which the boy now subscribes.

As the boy gets older, he may bloody his nose in a fight, become verbally hostile toward homosexuality, be driven to create an identity within a "pack" of other boys, and appear to cut the line connecting him to any mothering endeavors outside of servitude.

It's important to understand what is going on here. The boy is trying to prove to himself and his peers that he is 100 percent, grade A male. The pendulum must swing in this direction until he's sure of his own masculinity. The alpha male is his primary model until the issue of his own manhood is settled in his heart and mind. Only then can he relax and allow the pendulum to swing back a bit.

Perhaps you recall a huge pro football player named Rosey Grier. His hobby was needlepoint, a female-tinted endeavor if ever there was one. Rosey could come out publicly and declare his love for needlepoint. He could even have photos taken of him holding up the latest creation he stitched. But Rosey only had the luxury of doing so because his manhood was so unquestionable.

Before a boy will allow himself to explore compassion, tenderness, nurturing, and other values that real men need to develop, he must first be entirely sure of his own manliness.

Outside the home, the Christian church is the primary place where a boy should learn to be a man (see Psalm 34:11, Proverbs 20:7, and 2 Timothy 3:15). The Christian community ought to be the crucible in which the boy-into-man transformation takes place, but that church may need to rethink and retool many of its expectations, actions, and ministries if it is to be successful.

Godly men, who are willing to act, can make a wonderful difference in the life of a boy, especially during those years of transition between childhood and manhood.

Ancient cultures, both pagan and God-worshiping, have seen the importance of these transition years in the life of their boys. These years often become the starting point for accountability and instruction in behavior fitting for a man. They saw that in order for a man to emerge, the boy must rid himself of childish dependencies. In order to help boys do this, ancient men set a criteria for manhood and then required a boy to meet that criteria so that he could come through the fire into manhood. The idea of a heated testing to refine us is obvious in Scripture:

> And no one can ever lay any other real foundation than that one we already have—Jesus Christ. But there are various kinds of materials that can be used to build on that foundation. Some use gold and silver and jewels; and some build with sticks and hay or even straw! There is going to come a time of testing at Christ's Judgment Day to see what kind of material each builder has used. Everyone's work will be put through the fire so that all can see whether or not it keeps its value, and what was really accomplished. (1 Corinthians 3:11-13, TLB)

In a similar way, those cultures that impose a scorching but loving measure of what it means to be a man find that boys who have passed through that fire become men . . . or *better* men because of it.

It's my desire that the church will awaken to the fact that many boys are hopelessly adrift in their search for an invigorating manhood and that through some deep soul-searching and risk taking, the church will find a way to be a dangerously attractive and yet biblically solid entrance to that kind of manhood.

It is within the pages of Scripture that we find the defining characteristics of a man of God. We draw our standards of manhood from the examples set by heroes of the faith and our Lord himself. It's only through the Holy Spirit that men are able to live in the fullness of what God wants to do within their masculine souls.

Operating properly, the church should be able to teach and model these things in an attractive way to boys who want to become men. It's the role and duty of the church, working in harmony with a boy's natural family, to be a place that produces men, is attractive to men, and celebrates godly masculinity.

If we stumble in this mission, we unwittingly contribute to the damage rogue males searching for their manhood cause to our woman and our society.

I fear we have stumbled, and I fear we have much work to do.

Huckleberry was cordially hated and dreaded by all the mothers of the town, because he was idle and lawless and vulgar and bad—and because all their children admired him so, and delighted in his forbidden society, and wished they dared to be like him.

—Mark Twain
The Adventures of Tom Sawyer

2 GELDINGS AND STALLIONS

I thought our next-door neighbor had gone nuts.

A successful, middle-aged family man who just happened to be a top-rated chef at a five-star hotel, my friend never seemed to be the type Western movies were made of. So it came as quite a shock when the beefy new truck and the horse trailer showed up in his driveway. There he was, outfitted in a Stetson and snakeskin boots, and cinching up a lasso.

The chef had become a cowboy.

"Look," I said. "I wanted to be a cowboy once too, but I got over it."

My neighbor smiled at me knowingly and invited my kids to come ride with his family down at the meadow.

Thus began my education about horses.

Hanging over the corral fence, I was introduced to Butch.

Butch was my neighbor's horse. Batik was the horse that belonged to his wife. And Batik was pregnant.

"Hmm, guess Butch snuck into the corral at night," I said with a sly smile.

"Nope," said the neighbor. "Butch is a gelding. I had to have Batik studded. Cost me five hundred dollars."

"Five hundred dollars to have a horse do what I assume most male horses would happily do for free?" I asked ignorantly. "Gee, aren't there a whole bunch of guy horses around that would have been more than willing to spend the night with Batik for an apple or handful of hay or something?"

"Boy, you sure don't know anything about horses," he said with a laugh. "Most male riding horses are 'cut' when they are young. Only a few are left the way God made 'em. They're the stallions. They're wild, unpredictable, dangerous, and hard to tame. They're so rare that you have to pay a stud fee for putting them with your mare."

I smiled feebly and patted the docile and now pathetically named Butch. "Sorry for you, old boy. Guess you don't know what you're missing."

On the way home from the meadow, while the kids attempted to leverage us into buying them a horse (I told them to get a job and buy one themselves, which shut them up as they are only eight and ten years old), it occurred to me that the church has done a pretty good job of creating geldings as well.

Where are the stallions in our churches? How many wild, unpredictable, strong, aggressive, and somewhat dangerous males are deeply involved in the community of faith? We probably can't count very many within our ranks.

The church is simply not a good place for the likes of a stallion.

Consider a young boy who clearly manifests stallion material. He's hard to control, easily bored, straining to be physically unfettered from the confines of the classroom. He rears, he bucks, and if he stampedes, he draws the other little stallions with him.

Those given the unenviable job of overseeing stallions often have little tolerance for their wild and aggressive nature. For many church workers, these boys aren't seen as stallions at all but rather as troublemakers, pests, rabble-rousers, and undesirables to be broken or rid of. Some of these poor kids are diagnosed by adults as having "attention deficit disorder" or being "hyperactive" and are drugged into compliance.

The church imposes conformity to current societal expectations upon these wild and unruly boys, and those who resist are quickly diagnosed and anesthetized . . . for their own good, of course. Reprehensible, yet common even in Christian circles.

From the start of his church experience, the typical boy gets the strong message that this is no place for a stallion; thus, the stallions leave in droves. And we end up with lots of girls and a few geldings.

The Bible is a book filled with men who are stallion material. Consider the tragically flawed but oddly likable Samson.

With a divine gift of massive strength and the Holy Spirit stirring in him, Samson cut a path of fear and terror across the Philistine neighborhoods. It was his unpredictability coupled with unusual strength that made him dangerous. Here was a man, called and set aside by God, who combined cleverness, guts, and raw muscle into a divine message for the idol-groveling Philistines. This is the stuff of heroes.

Consider this biblical account of Samson's early career. It's tinged with enough testosterone to make it politically incorrect, yet here it is:

> When her son was born they named him Samson, and the Lord blessed him as he grew up. And the Spirit of the Lord began to excite him whenever he visited the parade grounds of the army of the tribe of Dan, located between the cities of Zorah and Eshtaol. (Judges 13:24-25, TLB)

Can you see the picture? Can you envision the military pomp and power of this Hebrew tribe connected with something God was preparing this little stallion for? It's easy to imagine a small Samson happily playing war, pouncing on his siblings, and wrestling neighborhood kids after a visit to the parade grounds. You can almost imagine his mother whispering her concerns: "We probably shouldn't take Samson down to the military grounds anymore; it really seems to rile him up."

But the wild excitement rippling in Samson was God induced, God programmed, God designed.

The story gets worse. Now the stallion is past puberty and God wants to use him in a unique and unconventional way.

> One day when Samson was in Timnah he noticed a certain Philistine girl, and when he got home he told his father and mother that he wanted to marry her. They objected strenuously.
>
> "Why don't you marry a Jewish girl?" they asked. "Why must you go and get a wife from these heathen Philistines? Isn't there one girl among all the people of Israel you could marry?"
>
> But Samson told his father, "She is the one I want. Get her for me."
>
> His father and mother didn't realize that the Lord was behind the request, for God was setting a trap for the Philistines, who at that time were the rulers of Israel.
>
> As Samson and his parents were going to Timnah, a young lion attacked Samson in the vineyards on the outskirts of the town. At that moment the Spirit of the Lord came mightily upon him and since he had no weapon, he ripped the lion's jaws apart and did it as easily as though it were a young goat! But he didn't tell his father or mother about it. Upon arriving at Timnah, he talked with the girl and found her to be just what he wanted, so the arrangements were made. (Judges 14:1-7, TLB)

As you read the rest of the story about this frustrated marriage attempt, an astonishing picture emerges of a tempestuous bull, saturated in male desires and strength, plowing through the ranks of the enemy, all under the direction and hand of God. It is a picture of a wild man being used by God—a man whose calling would necessitate his walking a tightrope over the burning fire of his lusts.

But it's also the hero's tendency to lose his spiritual and physical momentum to a nicely curved and perfumed shape that makes Samson a character that most men can identify with. His inability to rein in his desires leads to his demise. Men can relate to that.

It's the same problem the parabolic comic book character Superman had. The thing closest to home was the thing that could kill him. In the comic book, it was any chunk of his lost birth planet. In Samson's case, it was his emotional weakness and physical cravings.

We all recognize deep down inside the weakness we have for our own form of "kryptonite" and how dangerously close to it our journey sometimes takes us.

At the end of his life, Samson was able to call up the strength his foolishness had squandered in order to literally "bring down the house" of the Philistines. This is what redeems his hero status.

One cannot imagine Samson lasting long in a typical children's church.

As you thumb through the Bible, names of men who fit the stallion role spring out from the pages.

Moses, who as a young man bucked against the cruelty of Egypt, was called back into action after attempting to lead a "normal" life in the backwaters of the kingdom. While not as flamboyant as Samson, Moses turned out to be a tenacious opponent, flinging off every attempt of Pharaoh to bring him into submission.

Can you see the stallion in Daniel and his friends, who would not be tamed even by the most powerful of kings? Or in Joseph, who out of honor to God and his master pushed away the lusty advances of his boss's wife, only to be blamed by the scorned woman for attempted rape? Keep turning the pages and you will find stallions there in large and small print—the fiercely loyal warrior named Uriah upstaging in honor his compromised boss David, and in the same episode Nathan the prophet, bravely extending the bony finger of blame for Uriah's murder at David.

And what about the prophets and New Testament men who stood bravely silhouetted against the spiritual geldings of their day?

A righteous man's strength was found not just in the muscular exertions of the battlefield or in dangerously confronting hostile royalty, but also in quiet, determined ways. It was found just as much in saying yes to God as it was in resisting evil.

We pay lip service to the "mighty men of God" but are much better at culling out the mighty and leaving the meek.

The Christian church needs stallions desperately. We already have our fair quota of meek.

The church needs to be a place where those who love a challenge will find it, where those who become easily restless are liberated, and where the spirit that rears up inside these boys is not seen as a threat but as a symbol of strength.

Identifying the symptoms is easy. Acknowledging the disease is not much more difficult. Finding the cure and taking the prescription . . . now *that* is much harder.

Suppose we realize the need for a change. What can be done? How can we attract and inspire stallions?

The place to start is to recognize the stallions we have. This is fairly easy; just ask the Sunday school teachers to point out the troublemakers in class. There's a good chance that these are the strong male leaders who are merely leading in the wrong direction.

The next step is finding someone who isn't fearful of this wild bunch to take on the duty of directing their enthusiasm, leadership, and energy in a profitable direction.

Creative thinking is important at times, especially with boys who are a bit older. Acknowledging the obvious can be particularly helpful.

When Chris first came to our junior high group, it was like we'd been hit by a hurricane. The boy was thick in body, athletic, and aggressive. His ear-to-ear smile, good humor, and excitement acted as a magnet for the other boys. Chris was, from the moment he stepped into the room, clearly in command of the troops.

Adult leaders can react to this in different ways. Some actually become intimidated by these sawed-off leaders. Some decide to go toe-to-toe with them in order to establish who is boss. I decided to outthink the little ball of fire. I would attempt to give him a sense of responsibility and ownership. I would try to win him to my side by acknowledging what was already obvious to everyone: he was a leader.

Besides, it's much better to have a stallion pulling *with* you than pulling *against* you.

One day, during a break in activity, I pulled Chris to the side and whispered in his ear, "Hey, thanks for being here. I noticed that the other kids really look up to you, and I could sure use your help in making sure that everyone listens and does what they're supposed to."

Chris, who was tense at first (probably from a number of unpleasant confrontations with adults), brightened at my suggestion that we become a team and nodded in anxious agreement. He took charge like a drill sergeant, and in spite of a few bumps along the way, he is still, a dozen years later, involved in the church.

Adults may not be able to outrun young stallions, but they can usually outthink them.

During my long tenure in youth work, I made it a practice to go after the wildly energetic and wonderfully dangerous boys in our area. They would show up en masse, chewing up the landscape and any docile kid who stood in their path.

Anytime our youth group mixed it up with other churches, we'd often encounter gap-mouthed responses from other group leaders as they watched these middle-school barbarians mowing down their quiet, passive kids. It was like inviting Attila the Hun to a church picnic.

I must admit, it took some real creativity to channel the boundless energy, or at least dam it up temporarily, so that these boys could function in civilization.

One time, this powerhouse of male testosterone landed at a church winter camp. It had been a long bus ride and the boys were full of pent-up energy and ready to wreak havoc on the camp and campers alike. The electricity of their taut muscles crackled in the cold air. I had to think of something quickly to take the edge off.

It was then that I spotted a tall, stately pine tree at least six hundred yards away, rising magnificently from the top of a forty-five-degree hill.

As the animals piled off the bus, I gathered them around me and then pointed to the tree and shouted, "Five bucks to the first guy to touch the tree!"

Off they roared, pushing, shoving, and clamoring over each other. A literal herd of wild boys panting in the high altitude for a five-dollar prize. Some had no idea what they were running for. They just saw everyone take off and joined in the stampede.

By the time the boys staggered off the hillside, their pent-up energy was shot and they had become a manageable herd. At least for the time being. All it cost me was five dollars.

Naturally, working with the stallions will bring misunderstanding and controversy. Church leaders don't understand that it's not within the power of a youth worker to tame these kinds of boys at will in order to have them sit quietly during a church service or some other event designed for the passive learner.

The nonmalicious damage the herd is capable of doing to a church facility is frightful and right from the start it scares off many who are considering work with this kind of group.

A small church that heard about our aggressive, guy-oriented ministry asked me to meet with its board as a consultant so they could see if chasing stallions was a direction they might take as well.

We had our meeting in a large old hall with beautiful windows of paned glass and a nicely kept wooden floor. As it was the only long, wide room in the church not cluttered with pews, it was also the perfect place to do stuff with boys.

When I was given the opportunity to speak, I first explained the wonderful potential for a church that would be willing to go after the vast group of unwashed boys roaming the neighborhood. I shared stories of formerly fear-causing boys who were now leading dynamic Christian ministries because someone had reached out to them. I spoke of the future of the church and the need for exciting new blood. They were warm and receptive . . . even anxious. Then I dropped the other shoe.

Pointing to various windows, I said, "If you get our kind of youth ministry here, you can count on that window having a ball fly through it and that window to be on the receiving end of a broomstick." Some of the board members almost fell out of their chairs. I continued to prepare them by pointing to the wood floor and saying, "You can also figure that there will be some pretty deep gouges on this floor and maybe some stuff spilled on it that you'll have a hard time getting up." (Yes, it was a bit of overkill, but I wanted to see how they would react to even the possibility of those accidents happening.)

The board thanked me for my time and quickly tabled the discussion of developing youth ministry to boys.

Frankly, the church doesn't have stallions because it doesn't want stallions. They damage our goods, threaten our leaders, intimidate our pliable gentle students, dismantle the current pecking order, scare parents (particularly of girls), and raise our insurance premiums. They're noisy, boisterous, driven, and tricky to control.

Work with stallions and you'll end up taking lots of trips to the hospital. You'll find yourself trying to explain how the church steeple was turned into a rappelling course and where the cake for the women's lunch has disappeared to, plus a host of other nightmares.

Anything that's broken, missing, or left dirty will be attributed to the stallions, probably with some justification. (Stallions have to be broken and trained without being emasculated. It's a messy process.)

As long as the typical church wants to play it safe, put church facilities and things above people, and protect the status quo from the savages swirling outside its gates, there will be no place for these wild and wonderful leaders of tomorrow.

But with the help of someone who has insight into these kinds of boys, plus a little time, a stallion can be molded into a great leader and a productive member of society.

My friend and surf buddy Ken is a stallion. He's a perfect example of what *can be* if wisdom and understanding are applied to the life of a charger.

Compact, rugged, and clearly an ADD case, he must have been a handful as a kid, brawling his way through life.

Had Ken grown up today, he would have been quickly drugged into compliance just so that his schoolteachers could survive.

Fortunately for him, Ken had teachers who understood what kind of boy he was, a brilliant but restless kid who could easily focus on multitasking endeavors but could not sit still for five minutes.

Ken got as far as medical school. It was there that he ran into a dilemma. Medical school required hours of in-class lecture, but Ken couldn't sit in class for those extended periods without climbing the wall.

Ken approached a professor and explained his situation. He asked that a fellow student be allowed to tape the lectures, and he promised that he would listen to them while he was doing other things (such as working to support his wife and put himself through school). If his test scores were low, Ken promised he would attend class in person. The professor wisely took the bait.

Headset on, Ken would listen to the med school lectures while lifting weights, working, and driving the car. He aced his tests.

Ken is currently an emergency-room doctor, a profession that fits his stallion temperament to a tee!

Each stallion is a little different. Each requires special handling. But in time they can all make pretty good leaders in the temporal world and, as they submit to the strong hand of the Master, the eternal world as well.

These adult stallions demand and receive respect from the younger ones of their own kind. Not only that, but their company is attractive to many men who long to feel the wildness and godly danger again in their lives.

Numerous times in The Chronicles of Narnia, C. S. Lewis describes Aslan (representing Christ) as "not a tame lion." In addition, he emphasizes that not in any way is Aslan "safe."

Lewis was, as usual, brilliantly perceptive. The God of the universe is anything but tame or safe. He is wild and dangerous. He bucks at our attempts to bridle and control him. It should not be surprising that there is a godly wildness and danger bristling about those who are connected to him.

God-breathed imagination and creativity are available to be poured into the willing recipient. An energy that breaks the status quo should be expected when the spirit of the One who overturned tables pulses through the veins of men who serve him.

Obviously, all men are *not* stallions or even potential stallions of the sort that I'm describing. Manhood covers a spectrum of temperaments.

Yet the vast majority of boys, regardless of their ability to compete in a brawny world, are searching for that bridge that allows them to cross over to manhood, be recognized by other men, and be saluted by their peers.

For some budding men, every bridge to manhood is closed and barred in their high school years. But many do find the bridge a little farther down the river of life.

Tommy was a perfect example of this kind of boy.

By anyone's standard, Tommy was a cerebral but terribly geeky kid. Eleventh grade found him small, weak, and timid. Except in math and science, where he excelled, the boy was a clumsy, goofy sort of male failure. He was seen as a Y-chromosome accident in ill-fitting slacks and thick-framed glasses.

Tommy was not disliked; he was merely invisible. He simply didn't show up on the radar screen of high school manhood. In a man's world, someone like Tommy did not exist.

I came to know Tommy after my conversion to Christ in tenth

grade. An increased understanding of godliness had pushed me to reach out to those who were "the least of these" on campus. Because Tommy was a hopeless geek and fit the definition of "the least of these," I invited him to leave the solitude of his private lunch and join the "guys" at a lunch table studded with surfers, class officers, and athletes. He always accepted the offer but was clearly uncomfortable, a minnow among the sharks (even though they were mostly Christian sharks).

After graduation, my fellow classmates and I scattered like wind-whipped leaves. It wasn't until our ten-year reunion that I met Tommy again. And I didn't recognize him.

Tommy pulled up in a flashy sports car. A late growth spurt had added at least a foot to his height, and although many of the school jocks were starting to thicken around the waist, Tommy had developed the loping muscles of a distance runner. His hair, once a disorganized mix of cowlicks and dandruff, was now groomed and styled. He was dressed in expensive, well-cut clothes, and on his arm was a stunningly beautiful woman.

He called my name, broke into a smile, and waved his long arm. I had no idea who this guy was, but I waved back stupidly.

As it turned out, Tommy had used that math brilliance to land a job in the emerging field of computer electronics. He had become a successful and wealthy man. Somewhere along the line, Tommy had found a bridge he could cross. He was playing on par or better than par with those who had once imagined him to be a hopeless case. He had become a stallion—a breed of a different sort, but a stallion all the same.

What was true about Tommy is true about every boy on the male spectrum. They each need to cross into manhood. They need to find a way to let the stallion inside break out. Boys understand who are stallions and who are not. And they long to join the stallions on the run.

They were brave warriors, ready for battle and able to handle the shield and spear. Their faces were the faces of lions, and they were as swift as gazelles in the mountains.

(1 Chronicles 12:8)

3 A CAUSE, A HERO, AND A FLAG

I've often wondered what would happen today if a woman were to look out her window and see a seven-year-old boy prowling through the bushes, weighed down under a genuine army helmet, authentic ammo belts, and a sloshing canteen, and carrying an actual weapon.

Certainly the cops would be called and social services alerted, and the miniature gunman and his parents would be faced with hours of professional counseling. The evening news would make the incident scandalous.

Yet my mom and all the other neighborhood moms saw this sight often while I was growing up. In fact, Mom saw *whole troops* of pint-size GIs creeping slowly and quietly through her hydrangea bushes while scouting for the enemy. The young soldiers would keep up the hunt until an imaginary shoot-out occurred or Mom called them in for vanilla wafers and Kool-Aid, whichever came first.

Like the other children of World War II veterans, the boys in our house were expected to become warriors. Our parents looked upon it as psychological conditioning for what might in the future become a duty.

In the mid-fifties, army surplus stores were practically giving away the excesses of war. This meant that every kid who wanted to play army could be outfitted cheaply with the real gear, including a steel helmet. (Most of us found it much too heavy and wore the liner instead.)

I was particularly lucky in that a neighbor gave me a real World War II Japanese rifle (minus the firing pin), a war souvenir he had brought back from his tour of duty. It was heavy and oversized for my young frame, but I prized it because, unlike the plastic Tommy guns slung around by my friends, it had a lethal history. It had seen the very action we played at.

We would prowl through the neighborhood all morning, making the world a safer place by reenacting the deeds of our parents. It didn't matter that I was from a German family (it was my mom's first language) and that the guys across the street were from a Hawaiian/Japanese family—we were *good* Germans and *good* Japanese. We were all good guys, fighting for truth, justice, and the American way!

Once in a while we would let girls play. They were *always* nurses. Sometimes a kid would swipe a bottle of ketchup from the pantry to make sure that the victims had plenty of gore. Shaking it all over the victim's face and then dragging him to the first aid tent to hear the girls scream was the best part.

In the afternoon, tiring of make-believe conflict, we would choose up sides, dig dirt clods out of an embankment and, using trash-can lids as shields, meet in the alley for battle. Dirt-clod wars were exciting because the missiles exploded furiously upon impact but could be hurled like rocks. And for the most part, they didn't hurt too much.

The fun would usually go on until some kid got whacked in the eye and ran home crying. When the outraged mother would try to find the culprits in the alley she would discover that the warriors had evaporated into the arching sun, leaving only a few battered trash-can lids scattered about as evidence.

On rainy days we would launch an endless series of conflicts featuring immovable plastic soldiers, or we would contrive battles starring rope-swinging cowboys and hatchet-wielding Indians.

I had saved some money and sent away for a unique set of little plastic guys offered on the back of a comic book. I was the only guy on the block who had a play set of Custer's Last Stand.

In my play world, Custer was always the last to die, but faithful to at least *some* element of history, die he always did!

Occasionally someone would show up with a brick of elementary school gold: firecrackers. We'd quickly unstring the contraband explosives and divide them up like treasure among greedy pirates.

For the next week, we'd conduct countless experiments in power. I still recall the juicy results that answered the question "What would happen to a tangerine if you lit a firecracker inside it?"

The explosions tended to unnerve our moms, so we had to take our experiences to vacant fields, where each crack of violence was met with giddy laughter.

As the boys in the neighborhood aged, the battleground became a playing field, gym floor, or crowded surf spot. The uniforms changed color and style but always functioned to tell everyone what side you were on.

These antics were considered natural and normal for boys, as were tree climbing, fort building, bug tormenting, marble shooting, fire worshiping, BB gun toting, mud wallowing, and a host of other adventures that kept every kid busy until the streetlights went on. Even the suggestion that a boy would grow up to be a twisted, violent adult because of his immersion in these activities would have been scoffed at. Our parents, fathers in particular, would never allow us to be emasculated because some worried community group or social worker thought our activities should be taboo.

These memories are not the remains of some golden age of boyhood. They still resound in boys today. In spite of the best efforts of those in today's "helping" services, boys still find a way to be warriors. The surplus-store armies may be gone, but there are always new breeds of combatants to enlist.

In households where play guns are forbidden, little boys fashion rifles from sticks and die horrifying "deaths," plunging off the bed into a pile of pillows.

The desire to be a warrior wakes at some point in the heart of most boys. That desire seeps through the cracks and creases of any wall erected by those who think the solution to the woes of the world can be found by repressing this urge in boys, a desire that for centuries would have been considered naturally boyish.

All boys are practicing for battle. Somewhere, hardwired into those little male frames, a voice is whispering about the need to become a warrior. At a certain age, the whisper becomes a call and then a shout.

It's a call that never quite leaves the man. The warrior is the common element in "guy flicks" and many normal, nonviolent men deeply enjoy reading war history. Some reenact battles in authentic dress. Millions more tune in to brutal games of contact sports without fear that they are in need of therapy.

It would be easy to confuse the call to be a warrior with sin that came from the Fall. The sin from the Fall is what brings out the necessity of a godly warrior. In fact, it is God himself who ordains and empowers the warrior.

> He gives me skill in war
> And strength to bend a bow of bronze. (2 Samuel 22:35, TLB)

There will be a day when a warrior's impulse is no longer needed. That will be the same day sin is abolished from the earth forever. In the meantime, men understand that their warrior instinct is not something to be ashamed of, but that it should be encouraged and managed in an honorable way.

Living in a nuclear age has extinguished the ancient need for rallying an army to protect the village from vandals or Vikings. But every man still hears the call to be a warrior. Perhaps this means defending someone against a thug; perhaps it will involve taking heroic action in a life-threatening situation. Perhaps it will mean simply standing up for our kids when someone tries to trample their spirit or bully them.

Most men know that we must train and hone the aggression that is part of our nature. We know that we may be called on to use that aggression to battle an evil that may threaten us . . . or our loved ones.

Warriors go to war primarily to protect. If we're men, we're called to protect. It comes with the territory.

When something crashes downstairs in the middle of the night, it's usually the man who picks up the baseball bat or golf club and creeps down the stairs.

It's hard to imagine any man pulling the covers up around his ears and, in a quivering voice, saying to his wife, "You go see what it is!"

While practicing to be a warrior is exhilarating and even fun, actually confronting evil is a terrible and frightening duty.

We're warriors because we are programmed to be by God and expected to be by the world.

Not that this is popular thinking in all quarters of our society. Some go to extreme efforts in their attempt to expunge the warrior concept from boys.

Just ask the staff of the Kids Gym Schoolhouse in Wilmington, North Carolina. This preschool was docked points in its attempt to earn an endorsement by a state child-development supervisor for having "violent" toys available for the kiddies to play with.

The toys in question were not guns, grenades, switchblades, or ninja stars. They were nine little green plastic army men.[5]

As the offended supervisor explained, "They don't enrich the environment and can be potentially dangerous if children use them to act out violent themes."

Dangerous to whom?

Warriors *are* dangerous. They need to be in order to keep evil at bay.

In spite of all the uproar, we men still pick up the baseball bat at the sound of a bump in the night and still step into harm's way when it's demanded of us. Even in times of peace, there's always some context in which men need to be warriors.

Most men are rational enough to be able to transfer their aggression and competition into productive efforts. A man starts a business, and his unstated hope is to beat the competition and capture the market. A man goes to work for a company and he wants to succeed—become indispensable, elevated. This usually means that he must battle (with his wits and energy) an opponent. He feels especially satisfied when he beats out another man for a position or helps his company succeed. He wants to win. He is willing to fight, to draw economic blood.

Rather than returning from battle with his competitor's head on a stick, the modern business warrior brings home a larger paycheck or a bonus.

His family celebrates his efforts.

A man battles in other ways as well. He battles against other suitors for the affection of a woman.

He battles at the pickup basketball game, on the green, on the ice, in the field, or in a surf lineup with others. While a man remains focused on beating his opponent, it's usually in a good-natured way, for experience has shown him that bad sportsmanship is belittling.

[5] Victoria Rouch, "Tempest in a Toy Chest," *Wilmington Star,* November 15, 2001.

This does not mean that women are passive in the workplace or lack competition on the playing field, but there is a quantitative difference.

When someone gets hurt on my daughter's soccer team, the whole game grinds to a halt (with or without the ref's whistle). The girls of both teams often gather with hand-wringing concern around the wounded player and help escort her off the field. The game is resumed with a distinct sense of politeness and gentleness.

On my son's soccer team, a wounded player is left to drag himself off the field while the game goes on around—or over—his sorry carcass. Both teams are playing to win, but one is playing as if their lives were dependent upon it.

This kind of difference shouldn't alarm us. It doesn't suggest that something is wrong or out of kilter with either gender. God built women to be highly tuned to the relational end of the game and men to focus on scoring the goal or fighting the battle. The difference is factory designed. (See Genesis 3:16 as an example of how God designed men and women as two unique models.)

Men often see things (like a soccer game) from the framework of a battle.

Participating in a battle of some kind or preparing to do battle consumes the thoughts and time of most boys and men.

Not all wars are fought with physical violence. Sometimes the warrior wins by outthinking his opponent.

As a skinny kid, I found out quickly that fighting after school was not a winning proposition for me. I decided to find another method to defeat my enemies. Instead of my fists, I would use my tongue.

I became adept at razor-sharp put-downs and casual comments that would dissect my opponents before they realized what had happened. It was a warfare of wits, and I was a ruthless member of those special forces who fearlessly stand toe-to-toe with their adversaries . . . as long as they can choose the weapons.

THE BIBLICAL WARRIOR

The Bible is filled with stories of the brutal necessity of a warrior. When the Philistines (or Nazis, fascists, Communists, or militant Muslims) are thrashing their way into your homeland, the natural impulse is to run to arms. Much ink has been used in secular circles to lambaste the violence inherent in the Old Testament, yet the call to become a warrior "fighting the good fight" threads through biblical chapters, from the direct clashing warfare of King David to the metaphors that equate the Christian to a warrior, to gearing up and fighting a spiritual battle in the Epistles.

The Word of God beckons and calls out to the warrior hidden in each man. Some passages are drenched with military language, such as Paul's words to the church: "The weapons we fight with are not the weapons of the world. On the contrary, they have divine power to demolish strongholds" (2 Corinthians 10:4).

This is not to say that women are to ignore these muscular passages, but the imagery is clearly oriented to a male experience and resounds well with a man's impulses.

How the church decides to answer this call and whether or not it can provide the kind of leadership that inspires the fighter inside us tells us much about its present and future viability in the world of men.

The warrior needs a cause, a hero to lead and inspire him, and a flag to rally around.

A CAUSE

The cause worthy of a man needs to be righteous and true. Not all causes are worthy. The line that separates the cause of a pre–Civil War radical like the fiery abolitionist John Brown, whose attempt to ignite a slave uprising ended in carnage, and a reluctant emancipating warrior like Abe Lincoln, is a matter of degree. To find himself one of the "bad guys" feels like a dagger through the heart of a man. And it's equally tragic to the family and friends of the fighter. The ground of many battlefields is drenched with the misspent blood of warriors fighting for a cause that turned out to be unrighteous, even if the warriors were victorious.

At Masada, we don't celebrate the victorious Romans. Instead, we celebrate Jewish rebels who, by their own hands, ended their lives on top of a desert rock to spite the overwhelming power of their conquerors and hand them a hollow victory.

Not all causes are worth fighting for, nor are all men who find themselves in leadership trustworthy. Wars for expanded borders, nationalistic honor, or ethnic hatred have brought wretchedness and horror throughout history, and they continue to do so today.

The hero from whom the warrior draws inspiration must not be a despot but a man of deep character, truth, and honor.

While the call to be a warrior comes naturally to most boys and men, the choice to pick up weapons must be made with much prayer, clarity of thought, and biblical guidance.

Righteous men must help boys wrestle through just causes. Righteous men must help them harness the impulsive and sometimes destructive energy of youth and submit it to godly wisdom.

Dietrich Bonhoeffer became a warrior with his pen, and he paid for his influence against the evils of Hitler's regime on the gallows. His difficult choices were prompted by a love for righteousness.

The famous World War I hero Alvin York agonized greatly over the issue of entering the war as a combatant. His eventual choice to become an infantryman—and to show the bravery that was to win him the Congressional Medal of Honor—was not made by impulse, patriotism, or thirst for vengeance. It was the result of his struggle to know what God's will was for him at that time.

Regardless of the worth of the other causes in competition for the heart and soul of a young man, clearly the cause of Christ outweighs them all.

Paul eloquently gives these marching orders:

> But all these things that I once thought very worthwhile—now I've thrown them all away so that I can put my trust and hope in Christ alone. Yes, everything else is worthless when compared with the priceless gain of knowing Christ Jesus my Lord. I have put aside all else, counting it worth less than nothing, in order that I can have Christ. (Philippians 3:7-8, TLB)

The cause is not building larger church buildings, taking over countries in the name of Christ, or defeating theological foes. It's accepting the dare to follow the Master wherever he might lead.

Genuine Christianity offers challenge. It's not pew-bound sanctity, but get-your-hands-dirty action. It demands self-control, sacrifice, risk, and courage. When it's allowed to have its voice, Christianity speaks in a language men comprehend.

A HERO

Every boy wants a hero. Time may have tarnished his image of the lone brave man charging into danger on his massive white stallion, but deep in every man's heart, he hopes that something might define him as *extraordinary*.

Gallant, courageous, determined, and utterly selfless—these are the raw materials we think of when we think of those extraordinary men who end up as heroes.

If we don't offer genuine heroes to our boys, they will invent them. Hollywood stars, whose contracts usually don't allow them to do any of their own stunts, will become heroes merely because they pretend to be heroes.

Heroics are not the material of everyday life. The opportunity to "play the man" often comes by surprise. But if that opportunity can be anticipated, a man's drive to step into that role can be astonishing.

Just prior to the outbreak of World War I, an Antarctic explorer named Shackleton advertised for men to be part of a crew on an adventure that "may end in death." His office had an avalanche of applicants, each hoping that being a part of this new exploration would give him heroic stature . . . either in success or failure.

As it turned out, the expedition evolved into an unbelievable tale of survival as their ship was crushed by ice.

Shackleton and his men managed to survive a brutal winter on an ice floe and a perilous journey to safety in two small boats across the freezing, open Antarctic Ocean.

Why would men so readily sign up to risk their necks for such things? The call to be heroic is a powerful lure to a man.

Risk, especially risk for a worthy cause, is one of the things that makes a hero.

If you ever visit Hawaii, you may notice a plethora of bumper stickers, most affixed to rusting, surfboard-laden cars, proclaiming "Eddie would go." This curious saying is a tribute to the courage of Hawaiian waterman Eddie Aikau.

Aikau was a lifeguard and big-wave surfer on Oahu's treacherous North Shore. Strong and confident in the water, Eddie wouldn't pull back on any wave . . . regardless of how big or how dangerous.

During the spring of 1978, Eddie was a crewman on the Hokule'a, a replica of an ancient Hawaiian sailing vessel that was making its way toward Tahiti. Somewhere in the Hawaiian channel, in stormy seas and gale-force winds, the boat overturned, casting all onboard into the water.

After a night of the crew members futilely trying to attract passing boats and planes with flares, Eddie Aikau volunteered to paddle his surfboard, which he kept on the Hokule'a, to get help. He had assessed the situation and realized that options were running out. Soon the prevailing currents would take them far out to sea and beyond the reasonable hope of rescue.

There was no restraining Eddie. He was determined to go, and if anyone could make the arduous paddle, it was this outstanding waterman.

He set off with a strobe light and a ring of oranges around his neck for what he estimated would be a twelve-mile paddle to the tiny island of Lana'i.

He was never seen again.

A passing boat later rescued the crew of the Hokule'a.

Eddie's willingness to risk—even to sacrifice his life—has made him a legend to other watermen around the world. Men push other men to go farther, to risk more, with three simple words: "Eddie would go!"

Our culture likes to demythologize heroes of the past by showing their feet of clay and debunking their heroic status altogether. While a realistic picture of heroes may be helpful, the elimination of true heroes has left us with only the illusionary remnants displayed in film, sports, music videos, and magazines.

One thing is for certain: It's rare that a young man finds his hero within the Christian community.

Now is the time for our churches to dig deep into their rich past and reclaim the heroic figures that dared and suffered in their efforts to serve Christ. Now is the time to create an environment where we can place in front of young men our own living legends: men who have struggled and been found faithful, men who have faced hardships unknown to youngsters today and come through them stronger and better.

This is not because heroes are lacking. It's primarily because we haven't discovered those heroes, exposed our children to them, or wrested them from deep in history to show their relevance today.

A FLAG

Every warrior gathers under a flag. The flag represents the cause and becomes the rallying point for heroes. It becomes the place where *real* manhood is discovered and developed.

Most schoolchildren know that the flag of the nation is always at the top of the flagpole, while the flags of the state and other organizations stack up below it. The meaning of the hierarchy is obvious: The nation comes before the state.

The "flag" of love and loyalty to Christ flies at the top of a warrior's life (see Mark 12:29). Other commitments and concerns stack up below it.

In the midst of a civil war, the Roman general Constantine, while not yet a Christian, claimed that a dream came to him on the eve of battle, showing a cross with an accompanying voice telling him, "By this sign, conquer." In the morning, by his order, the banner of the cross was raised, his men rallied, and the enemy was routed. Constantine became emperor of Rome and friend to the church.

The church Christ ordained, represented by numerous little congregations around the world, has a banner to fly—a banner to lead us into spiritual battle. It's not the banner of a denomination or worship style. It's the banner that will rally us to a common cause, a cause by which we will be able to conquer. " 'Not by might nor by power, but by my Spirit,' says the Lord Almighty" (Zechariah 4:6).

That flag—the supremacy and love of our Lord—still attracts men wherever it is raised above other causes.

The Christian ideal has not been tried and found wanting; it has been found difficult and left untried.

—G. K. Chesterton

4 WHY MEN DON'T GO TO CHURCH

When I was a kid, someone gave our family a picture of Jesus, and we hung him on our den wall. At least it was supposed to look like him. When you're a kid, you naturally assume that it does.

According to this artist, Jesus was a gaunt, pasty white creature hidden under mounds of flowing robes. His lengthy, pointed European nose made his eyes look dark and hollow; his hair was long, thin, and stringy. He was painted to look strained, tired, and supplicant.

Gentle Jesus, meek and mild. Soft and suspiciously effeminate.

As soon as I became aware of real manhood, I wanted nothing to do with this guy.

I would follow Davey Crockett all the way from the swamps

of Tennessee to swinging ol' Betsy at the top of the Alamo before I would follow the wimpy Jesus pictured in our den.

I began to believe that church was for guys who related to this weakling in the picture. In fact, it seemed to be a place for weaklings in general: kids, women, and men so whipped by life that they needed to hide out in the church. And in addition to the weaklings, church seemed the perfect place for misfits, weirdos, library jockeys, and other Quasimodos of this world.

The Christians I would say this to were quick to point out that the church should serve as a hospital for those banged up in life.

But nobody *wants* to stay in a hospital any longer than he or she has to. It's a place for the wounded to get well and then get going. Instead, it appeared to me that the church was a sanitarium where everyone was given medication but nobody seemed to be getting much better. "Normal" people might visit on Christmas or Easter, but they would never want to *live* there.

A lot of men feel as I did.

Even today, the majority of our churches come across to men as institutional, starchy, sanitized, and corny.

Even the guys running it seem to be doubtful candidates for manhood. Some of them run around in robes or odd-collared shirts. And if there are still any doubts, consider the scandalous sexual charges thrashing the leadership of the Catholic church.

The church seems to be a place for men of questionable manhood, not a place for future heroes.

The tragedy of this is that the church is created and headed by Jesus Christ himself. The Gospels confirm that this idea of the church today is a long way from the demanding and muscular faith that was demonstrated by its creator and his early followers. Consider some of the things he told his followers, and you'll see that our faith is clearly not for the faint at heart.

> Anyone who wants to be my follower must love me far more than he does his own father, mother, wife, children, brothers,

> or sisters—yes, more than his own life—otherwise he cannot be my disciple. And no one can be my disciple who does not carry his own cross and follow me. (Luke 14:26-27, TLB)

And he pointed out that it would take deep commitment. Quitter types were advised to not even start the journey.

> But don't begin until you count the cost. For who would begin construction of a building without first getting estimates and then checking to see if he has enough money to pay the bills? Otherwise he might complete only the foundation before running out of funds. And then how everyone would laugh!
>
> "See that fellow there?" they would mock. "He started that building and ran out of money before it was finished!"
>
> Or what king would ever dream of going to war without first sitting down with his counselors and discussing whether his army of 10,000 is strong enough to defeat the 20,000 men who are marching against him?
>
> If the decision is negative, then while the enemy troops are still far away, he will send a truce team to discuss terms of peace. So no one can become my disciple unless he first sits down and counts his blessings—and then renounces them all for me. (Luke 14:28-33, TLB)

Our Lord called out for a tough sacrificial lifestyle from those who wanted to follow him. No pillows, no porters.

> But Jesus replied, "Remember, I don't even own a place to lay my head. Foxes have dens to live in, and birds have nests, but I, the Messiah, have no earthly home at all." (Luke 9:58, TLB)

> Then Jesus said to the disciples, "If anyone wants to be a follower of mine, let him deny himself and take up his cross and follow me." (Matthew 16:24, TLB)

The church Jesus founded—the church pioneered by Peter, John, James, Paul, and Timothy—was invigorating to male sensibilities. It was attractive to men, and it was led and driven by men, tough men. They transformed their culture and left a high watermark for the modern church to measure itself by.

Has Jesus stopped leading men? Is the church of this decade not under the same leadership and direction as the church of history? Or has the church neglected God's guidance and, in the process, made itself unattractive to men?

There are a number of reasons men hesitate to darken the door of a church. Some are reflections of our culture; many are failures of the church to speak in the language of men. Let's look at a few of those reasons.

SUSPECT LEADERSHIP

Many men regard the masculinity of some full-time Christian workers with suspicion. Catholics in particular have it bad in this respect. (Protestants and Catholics may consider each other as apples and oranges in church and theological matters, but secular men don't make the distinction when they evaluate the relevance of church in their lives.)

Men have serious doubts about the masculinity of those who would voluntarily choose a life without women. Constantly erupting sexual scandals, many involving homosexual behavior, add to the skepticism.

Even those devoted to the Catholic church acknowledge the problem. Leon J. Podles, whose recent book *The Church Impotent* outlines with solid academia the weakness of male leadership in the Catholic church, gives a shivering description of his experiences in seminary: "I decided I might have a vocation in the priesthood and went to a pre-seminary at a men's college. (I was privileged to have a now-rare single-sex education for eight years.) As I discovered, the seminary, unfortunately, was full of homosexuality of various sorts.

The policy of the authorities was to ignore the situation, hoping it would go away. Whether it went away, I do not know, but I went away."[6]

Sadly, the response of most unchurched men is probably, "I suspected as much!"

Even though evangelicals have done better in this regard, especially with the success of movements like Promise Keepers, these efforts are largely parachurch, and their positive male imagery doesn't usually transfer over to the corner churches in our neighborhoods.

The sad fact is that the ranks of clergy—both Protestant and Catholic—are often filled with those who favor the more academic, malleable, and gentle end of the male spectrum. This doesn't mean that the leaders are not real men but that there is an important balancing element of masculinity not widely represented.

The perceived weakness within church leadership isn't helped when strong males can bully the clergy. Consider the case of the late John Gotti, a Mafia crime lord and unrepentant murderer who was given a church burial, a privilege in the Catholic church supposedly reserved for Christians in good standing with the teachings of the faith.

Evangelicals can see a similar caving in when men in leadership are afraid to stand up to a boisterous but influential member who demands his way (often at the cost of God's true vision for the church).

Once while visiting a friend's church, I noticed an enormous, rustic podium sitting awkwardly in the foyer. The massive piece of furniture seemed strangely out of place and useless except for holding discarded cups and remnants of last week's bulletin.

I asked my guide about the monstrosity and he rolled his eyes in exasperation.

It seemed that many decades ago, a member of the congregation who was now deceased had lovingly but, er, uh, ruggedly handcrafted

[6] Leon J. Podles, *The Church Impotent* (Dallas: Spence Publishing Company, 1999), 10.

this podium. Even though a new modern podium had replaced the old one many years ago, a particular family member would get very upset whenever the suggestion of discarding this one came up.

No one in leadership had the courage to get rid of the podium and so there it sat, a testament to weakness under the guise of peacemaking.

I've found this to be a ridiculously common occurrence in many churches.

The message for men? Power and money can blur issues of morality and derail the mere common sense of weak church puppets; so power and money have more strength for a man than anything the church might be peddling.

TOO MANY WOMEN

As a kid, there was little worse than the invasion of our home by a girl's slumber party. Even the name *slumber party* is an oxymoron when you put a gaggle of young adolescent females in the same room for the night.

From time to time, one of my sisters would claim the divine right—on the basis of a birthday or some other flimsy excuse—to have a slumber party. Soon, all of her twittering friends would arrive for the night, dragging crammed luggage, pillows, stuffed animals, boxes of nail polish and makeup to put on and take off all night (for no apparent reason), and bags of highly fattening food to be consumed as a sign of penance for complaining about how chubby their thighs had become.

As far as my brother and I were concerned, an invasion of fleas would have been preferable. For a while, harassing the girls was fun, but by 2:00 A.M., the chatter and giggling was still going strong and we began to feel as if we were drowning in estrogen fumes. There were just too many girls. We had to get out! We would pitch a tent in the yard and lay joyfully under the stars, content in the outdoors, where *men* belong, breathing the rich, unperfumed night air.

This is exactly how a lot of guys feel about church: It's a spiritual slumber party where the women call the shots and the guys play a background role. Or at the other end of the spectrum, men see the church as a cultic place where a few men who would be powerless in a real man's world get their jollies by abusing and ordering around sheepish women under the guise of God's will.

But mostly men see the church as full of women.

Having too many women in a group does not stimulate masculinity; instead, it suffocates it. While men enjoy women, they flourish in the company of men. They are with those who speak the same language, resound with the same sensibilities, share the same passions, and even understand and commiserate with rather than condemn dark urges.

Among women, a man is always on his guard. He tiptoes carefully around uncharted territory, hoping not to tread on a female land mine. Or he feels he must take on a role of some kind: the knight, the wise man, the joker. It's impossible for him to be one of the guys when surrounded by girls.

If he's around women for too long, especially if he seeks out their company or is incorporated into their world, the man becomes suspect to his peers. *Is he a Lothario, a wolf looking for a pretty sheep?* they wonder. *Has he abandoned masculinity and gotten in touch with his "feminine side"?*

Too many women tilt the balance of power—if not obviously, then subtly. Men feel themselves shrinking when it seems women are in control.

THE CHURCH IS PERCEIVED AS IRRELEVANT TO MEN

According to pollster George Barna, when it comes to the way we live our lives, there's not much difference between those who claim to be believers and those who don't.

This is just what most men suspect. People who go to church are just as good or just as lousy as people who don't. So why bother wasting time with something that makes no obvious difference one way or the other?

To the shame of the church, the kind of Christianity we've demonstrated has often not been convincing enough to attract men toward it.

Consider these statistics the Barna Research Group came up with about areas of vital importance to the Christian faith.

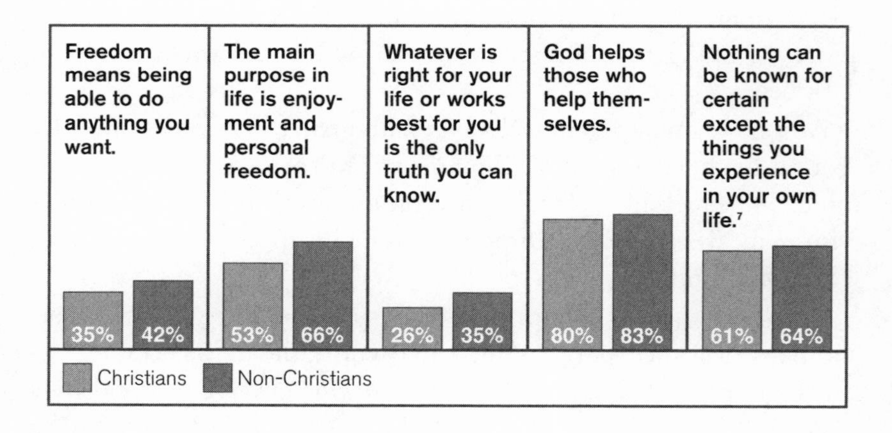

Note how the rate of agreement with these statements is nearly a dead heat between believers and nonbelievers. Christians get divorced at the same rate as unbelievers, hold the same values as unbelievers, and think in much the same ways as unbelievers. Barna delivers this biting summary: "After studying 131 different indicators of who we are as people, we concluded that it is difficult for non-Christians to understand Christianity since few born-again individuals model a biblical faith."

So why would a man find it necessary to go to church?

Men are generally pragmatic and practical. They're problem solv-

[7] George Barna, *Growing True Disciples* (Colorado Springs: Waterbrook Press, 2001), 77–79.

ers and solution finders. Many men see church as a bland, lukewarm society with no real relevance or agenda. If involvement in a church makes no functional difference in the quality of life—if it does not challenge, invigorate, or empower a man, why attend?

Women, too, dislike irrelevance. But women often will build a society or network of relationships that creates relevance for them. Since men are much slower to build relationships with other men, and since men in churches are not always present in great numbers, the exit sign usually is more appealing.

THE CHURCH IS AN INSIDE EXPERIENCE

Men (and boys) are basically outdoor creatures. Scan the magazine rack and you will find titles such as *Field and Stream, Guns and Ammo, Motor Trend, Sports Illustrated, Golf, Surfer, Outdoors,* etc. The two main things these magazines have in common is that they are aimed at and almost exclusively purchased by men, and they are all about interests that are done outside the house. While it's true that there are many women who enjoy the outdoors and men who are house bunnies, both experience and checkbook stubs prove that the outdoors is really a man's world.

Church is an inside experience. Therefore, there must be something more motivating than mere spiritual maintenance to make a man want to invest his free time in a church service.

At its origin, the church was filled with men who came inside to hear in order to go outside and "do." Christianity was ordained to be a lifestyle, not solely an inside experience framing an irrelevant lecture with music (often unsingable) and liturgy (frequently indecipherable).

Men were created to act and to lead. In the past, the lifestyle demanded by their master made them apparent in the communities in which they lived (hence the name "Christian"—little Christ). They lived hard, sacrificial, intentional, courageous lives.

If you had followed the apostle Paul around the Roman world, you could have said with him:

> I have worked harder, been put in jail more often, been whipped times without number, and faced death again and again and again. Five different times the Jews gave me their terrible thirty-nine lashes. Three times I was beaten with rods. Once I was stoned. Three times I was shipwrecked. Once I was in the open sea all night and the whole next day. I have traveled many weary miles and have been often in great danger from flooded rivers and from robbers and from my own people, the Jews, as well as from the hands of the Gentiles. I have faced grave dangers from mobs in the cities and from death in the deserts and in the stormy seas and from men who claim to be brothers in Christ but are not. I have lived with weariness and pain and sleepless nights. Often I have been hungry and thirsty and have gone without food; often I have shivered with cold, without enough clothing to keep me warm. (2 Corinthians 11:23-27, TLB)

If ancient church history is to be believed, the other early leaders' lives echoed many of the same hardships.

They lived effective, exciting, dangerous, thrilling lives. The Christian church burst on the scene as a radical alternative to the philosophies of the day, which were typified by men who sat, thought, and talked but did little else. The early church was markedly different, and it transformed the world as a result.

BUT DAD DOESN'T GO!

My father left the scene just as I was rising to adolescence. He was a successful family man and businessman who developed an unsuccessful relationship with the bottle, which resulted in the crashing down of all he had built in his life. His abandonment was more like a drift than a sudden departure. Like the tide, he slowly ebbed away. But he was around long enough to leave me with some solid memories, both good and bad.

Dad went to church for a while. "It makes your mom happy," he'd say. Then came a time where making Mom happy wasn't as important as sleeping in or tinkering with the boat engine.

Initially, Mom would pile the five of us kids into the family station wagon and take us to church. But in later elementary school, the tasteless Kool-Aid and store-bought vanilla snaps they served as a Sunday school "treat" didn't have the same draw as staying home to read the Sunday comics or getting my hands greasy in the garage.

As the oldest, I was the first to ask, "Why do we have to go to church?" I don't recall my mom's response, but I do recall my rebuttal: "But Dad doesn't go!"

My father was smart enough not to buck my mom on the church issue. "Go to church!" he'd growl. "It's good for you!"

I said nothing, but my mind spoke: *Yeah, right. If it is so "good for you" why do you hide out in the garage? I know what's going on. Church is for kids and moms, and you just don't think I'm grown up enough to be done with it.*

Dads everywhere give the message that Christianity isn't much of a priority to them. There are all kinds of other, more important things to do: golfing, fishing, hunting, going to the beach, watching sports on TV, hanging out at the local coffee emporium, shooting the breeze with the guys, messing around in the garage, finishing a project, or banging around in the workshop. These are the things that matter to many men.

Because young boys learn from example, they usually believe what they see more than what they're told. When they see the primary males in their lives eschewing Christian fellowship, even if they verbally suggest its value, boys know which message to believe.

THE CHURCH TENDS TOWARD INEFFICIENCY

Have you ever seen how men shop? With few exceptions, men will walk into a store, find the pants, shirt, shoes, dog food, car polish, or whatever they came for, try it on if need be, buy the same size in three colors, and be gone. Shopping for men is quick, efficient, and painful only to the wallet. The majority of men want to spend as little time in the mall as possible. "Let's go in, take care of business, and get out!" is our mantra.

This is why Tupperware parties and their ilk don't work with men. Can you imagine men showing up for a tool party? *Join us this Friday for chips, soda, and a fine selection of drill bits.* Well, maybe if there was soda, chips, cards, *and* drill bits.

For men, the Tupperware model is an extremely inefficient way of conducting business.

I'm told that Tupperware parties are so popular because they speak to a woman's desire for relationships (and, I suppose, more handy containers in which to keep stuff).

Men often see the church in the same light as a Tupperware party. It's a fun place for women but not a place men want to spend much time.

Men like institutions that *do* things rather than simply talk about doing things. Although many Christians insist the church is a living organism rather than an institution, this definition is usually lost or unheard by the typical man in our society.

Other groups and organizations are active and busy. Rotary Club, Lion's Club, Kiwanis, and the like lubricate business connections and raise cash for charities or build playgrounds for the community.

Churches, by contrast, are relatively nonfunctional and inefficient. We have church services, but we don't do much that would be of interest to most men.

We waste a lot of money, too. Churches build cavernous rooms at great expense that can only be used for one purpose. We put huge amounts of money into evangelistic efforts that reap very little results . . . and then justify our actions by declaring that you can't put a price tag on a soul. (This notion really doesn't fly with business men who expect to see something tangible for their buck.)

Considering our mandate to make disciples and spread God's message to the world, the church spends a great deal of time and resources patting each other on the back and entertaining ourselves, but very little on making connections with the community we say we are here to minister to.

Often, churches think in terms of defense. We see it as our role to filter out "the world" rather than engaging in it, to protect the flock from the secular world rather than preparing them to live in it. As a result, not much gets done that the average guy on the outside can see.

Men often see the church as a social or emotional place but not a *doing* place. Because men are *doing* creatures, they value *utility* above emotion.

For example, if a man becomes sick and is confined to the hospital, a bouquet of flowers would probably not be the best choice to send as a get-well token. Most men are somewhat nonplussed by flowers. A potted plant might be a better choice, because a man would likely reason that at least the thing could be stuck in the ground to enhance the yard after the hospital stay.

Better yet, you might consider a Venus's-flytrap, the ultimate flora in the male economy. Useful, efficient, industrious, practical, and for the fly, deadly! It's a plant that earns its living. Now *this* would really cheer up a hospitalized man!

Men often see the church as ornate, flowery, and perhaps even emotional. They rarely see it as a practical and efficient place to invest their time and energy.

THE CHURCH AVOIDS CELEBRATING MALE SEXUALITY

I will never forget the first time I read the Song of Songs. As a fairly new Christian and a senior in high school, I was astonished by the innuendoes that seemed to celebrate two lovers' physical passion in the marriage bed. No one had ever told me I could find that kind of stuff in the Bible, but here it was—the melding of the physical and the romantic. And it was blessed and considered holy.

"Let's have some teaching on *this* stuff!" I enthusiastically declared.

When someone finally became brave enough to tackle the book, I was dumbfounded. According to my teacher, the Song of Songs only *appeared* to be about passion. It was really about Christ and the church, I was told. Jesus was the handsome bridegroom, and the church was the panting bride. All those metaphors had significance only as seen through the lens of Christianity.

I didn't like this explanation at all. In fact, it felt kinda creepy. I had a hard time envisioning myself as the female in this book.

Rats! I said to myself. I thought the book was about a Hebrew couple that was "doing it" the right way. I had been hoping for some practical tips and some juicy commentary. Instead, I got theological babble.

And to be perfectly honest, while I now understand it from an academic point of view, I still have a hard time relating to imagery of the church as a bride and have happily returned to my initial instinct about the Song of Songs.

I suppose the same can be said for women who experience a similar discomfort with the military metaphors in Scripture, or for those people who grew up with a lousy father and find it tough to take comfort in God as their father. But I think that a lot of men feel the way I do about the Song of Songs.

Do you know what's the top-selling issue of any magazine aimed at men in America? *The Sports Illustrated Swimsuit Edition.*[8]

It's not about sports. It's about sex. Soft sex, but sex all the same. It sells because men think about sex . . . a lot. A lot more than we like or want to admit. This is true for most guys, even Christian guys.

[8] The *International Summary World Magazine Trends Handbook 2001/2002* by the International Federation of the Periodical Press, in their "Top 50 Special Interest Magazines by Circulation" category (p. 50), puts *Sports Illustrated* as the #2 highest-selling magazine in the world and #1 in the USA, of which the *Swimsuit Edition* is the highest-selling single issue.

In spite of some early mixed signals I received from the church, I've come to believe that God made us sexual beings. He made us sexually charged by design. Like anything else, the gift can be abused or misused, but in and of itself, the gift is good.

Without godly and frank male-based guidance, a man can easily begin to see women only as objects, divorcing sex from love, commitment, and responsibility. But only rarely is the male propensity for thinking about sex described as a good thing. In many churches, boys are told not to think about sex—if they're told anything at all—rather than taught *how* to think about sex.

The church needs to celebrate godly sexuality rather than be embarrassed by it. It should be a comfortable subject in our community, not a tawdry one. The church should redeem and rescue sexuality from the domain of hedonism. After all, it was God's idea first, and it works pretty well when we do it his way.

THE CHURCH IS SOFT

Many men see the church as soft, pudgy, toothless, and emasculating.

It often seems as if the church is working in collusion with a culture bent on emasculating men and turning raw male material into pliable, de-fanged images of its own liking. When challenged by our culture, the church rarely takes on a male voice or defends male sensibilities. In fact, it often chimes in with those who see male strengths as liabilities.

School districts in states such as Texas, Virginia, Massachusetts, and Maine have banned a particularly violent game from the school grounds.

The game is dodgeball. Also banned are the game's evil cousins with ominous names: poison ball, murder ball, killer ball, and burn ball.

According to the "experts," the game encourages the strong to pick on the weak and creates an environment where those who aren't as agile or quick end up sitting out most of the game. And of course, throwing any object at another human being fosters violence.

The fact is, while dodgeball utilizes the elements of skill, dexterity, and luck, the very thing that makes it delicious to boys is its violence. It's war with a red rubber ball. It's combat without a whole lot of bloodshed or bruises. While it is a war that girls can play, the real proponents of dodgeball are boys.

Banning dodgeball may only be a portent of things to come. A school in California has also eliminated the game of tag.

It seems that this evil game lowers the self-esteem of those who can't run as fast as the other kids. Darwin's "survival of the fittest" theory may rule in the science class, but it loses all its backers on the playing fields of these "enlightened" public schools.

Games that have a violent element, games that end up with winners and losers, games with any sort of competition are becoming targets for elimination by many elements in our society including churches, Christian camps, and Christian institutions.[9]

We think that by eliminating these sorts of games, we'll produce kinder men, but instead we're producing cream puffs.

And sadly, this assault on masculinity is sometimes championed by well meaning people in the church. (Not necessarily evangelicals, but certainly those in churches whose spiritual sensitiveness seem to track with the current political sensitivities.)

Competition in general has even become suspect. Somehow many Christian churches have been swept into thinking that there should be no winners or losers in life—that "everyone is a winner."

But there are losers. Sometimes it is the same loser over and over again. It is the sting of being a loser, the last picked, the rejected player—or the fear of being it—that often puts determination and character-building grit into a boy at the same time it wounds him.

Men instinctively know this "everyone is a winner" thinking to be

[9] Jody Veenker, "Moral Combat," *Christianity Today,* 6 March 2000.

untrue in the real world, but the assault on "Philistine" thinking continues. The softening effects become as silly as the Boston-area high school policy that has eliminated all references to valedictorian or salutatorian so that others won't have their feelings hurt.

Sadly, Christian churches are often taken in by this make-everybody-feel-good thinking and forget their duty to prepare boys for manhood. And the truth of the matter is this: Manhood involves lots of competition—sometimes even full-contact competition.

Many boys love to play paintball. After the first game I played with our high school group, I was hooked as well. Now I *love* to play paintball. Not the "charge across an open field and try not to get slaughtered" version of the game but the quiet, skulking version of it.

I find sneaking through the forest, hunting the other team, which is at the same time hunting my team, wildly exciting. Because those paint-filled balls come hurling at you with enough force to raise a serious welt, the game includes an element of pain and danger as well.

Because paintball attracts boys of any age, even many fathers—and of course, the pastor—in our church bought twenty guns, masks, and a fill station. We are now Paintball Central.

Other churches have a hard time with this. They suggest we're encouraging violence among males. One leader even prophesied that these boys would one day grow up to beat their wives.

I freely admit this sport panders to the warrior spirit. I have the welts to prove it. I agree that it draws out the aggressive nature in the guys who charge through the brush.

And I believe it makes kids a bit tougher and helps them learn courage, teamwork, and strategy. I would wager that most of the male domain would ditto this conclusion. Not only that, but we have discovered that there is no other single activity that draws more unchurched young males into contact with our church.

In the secular world, a church with a paintball team is seen as a place that's attractive to men and clearly complemented with male sensibilities.

The fact that a game of paintball is even an issue with some churches proves the point to many a man who believes that the church has joined the politically correct crowd and gone soft.

Now while this may not be your church, it's important to remember that the average Joe doesn't make the distinction between "types" of churches. He sees those emotion-driven churches flying from the rafters, those in cahoots with liberal culture, and those dressed in gold-threaded robes and swinging incense cantors as one in the same. Like it or not, we have a corporate identity.

The message the church often sends to men is this: "Enter our doors and we will emasculate you—in Christian love, of course."

It's no wonder men stay away.

Learn to do good, to be fair and to help the poor, the fatherless, and widows.

(Isaiah 1:17)

5 MAN HUNGRY

Halfway down the old road that leads from the raucous border city of Tijuana to the sleepy port town of Ensenda sat an orphanage known as *Hogar de Luce* (House of Light). Somewhat dilapidated and painted a gaudy bright red by a misguided group of Americans on a mission to paint something, the place housed four dozen or so scrubby kids and the Torres family, the orphanage's elderly founders.

Typical of most orphanages in Mexico, this one had few genuine orphans. Most of the kids were either unwanted or inconvenient. Many would be "visited" by their birth mother occasionally. Sometimes a mother might have several children in the orphanage but only pay attention to the one for whose father she had feelings. Often kids would be "reclaimed" by a parent when they were old enough to be put to work.

For several decades, until the old couple that ran the place died and it closed down, I had the privilege of visiting this small refuge on a monthly basis.

Usually I would arrive with a load of high school students in tow. Our pockets would be filled with marbles, rolls of caps (the kind that go off like a small bomb when the whole roll is whacked with a rock or hammer), little army men, tops, yo-yos, and candy. Needless to say, we were always met with great enthusiasm.

Some orphan lookout would spot my surfboard-laden van bouncing and billowing down the dusty road and give the alert, and within seconds, the rooms would spew children racing to gather around the incoming vehicles, chanting my name like a mantra.

One thing that struck me about the kids at this orphanage (and just about every other one I've ever visited) was the incredible sense of man hunger in the boys.

Once I'd alighted from my car, I'd find myself surrounded by small boys who wanted to feel my hairy arms and get burns from the stubble of my whiskers. Little arms would wrap around my neck, my legs, and my forearms. Even after my pockets were emptied of goodies, the boys clung to me and followed me like puppies. It was the same with every other man (and even the more adult-looking high school guys) we brought to the place. One hint of friendliness and the little boys would mob them.

When it was time to leave, the kids would beg us to come back tomorrow. We couldn't. Tomorrow we would be back with our families, rolling on the floor with our own children, while these children waited for the next group of men who would do more than drop off food supplies or patch the roof.

These were boys without the imprint of a man. They were desperately hungry for someone who could set the direction of their inner masculine compass. They were starved for touch . . . a man's rough, firm, and callous touch.

I've seen it many times before. I've seen it in the eyes of boys my own kids have brought home with them—boys who don't have a place to go to, an adult male to talk to, or a mentor to copy. Shepherdless sheep with first names like Donovan or James, who carry their mothers' last names instead of their fathers'. Kids without dads who come over to visit but are drawn to stay. Kids who end up with a drawer of their clothes at our house.

I've felt the hunger in my own heart.

What is it like to be fatherless? What is it like to have no idea how a man would react in a family situation? to never smell a man's cologne or his coffee-tinted breath kissing you good morning? to never prowl his office or bounce along in his truck? to never know his presence at a game? What is it like to have no one there to teach you the little details of life: how to tighten a screw (righty-tighty, lefty-loosey), how to lather up and shave, how to knot a tie, how to cast a lure and clean a fish, how to throw a ball, and what it means to still be romantic with your wife of ten years?

Among the problems of our modern culture, children who are fatherless as the result of divorce, casual partnering, or a woman's single-parent choice may prove to have the greatest negative repercussions of all. Without the help of their fathers, we are raising males who can't find their way to being men.

Recently, the journal *Nature* described a South African study of young bull elephants raised in a herd that had lost all adult male members. These fatherless juveniles were easily agitated. They became wild and destructive, killing and causing chaos at random. This is not typical elephant behavior, and destroying these violent youngsters seemed a likely option.

The wildlife managers captured the young beasts and shipped them off to a herd with a healthy population of adult males. The results were dramatic. The young bulls settled down as the older males began to imprint "correct male elephant behavior" onto them.[10]

What is true in the wild is also true in civilization. A boy without the imprint of a good man will join together with other boys and turn toward the brutal, twisted, and desolate.

[10] R. Slotow, G. vanDyk, J. Poole, B. Page, and A. Klocke, "Older Bull Elephants Control Young Males," *Nature,* Vol. 408, 23 November 2000.

An imprint of a godly man on the heart of a boy forms the contours and diagram of what he needs to become.

This, by the way, explains the reason gangs are so prevalent in urban cultures. The number of fatherless boys in an urban setting far exceeds that in the suburbs. The pull toward violence and cruelty is amplified in these situations.

No place in our culture has been harder hit from the absence of the male imprint than urban communities. Repeat teenage pregnancies and unmarried liaisons have produced streets filled with young boys desperate for a man's guidance.

Without nature to challenge; with limited places to release energy; without a father, grandfather, or positive male mentor, the boy views the streets as his proving ground. It's easy to see the lure of a gang's violent male bravado.

The wretched cycle of violence, sexual conquest, abandonment of children, substance abuse, and irresponsibility repeats itself over and over again. Hopelessness and, in spite of the male posturing, a sense of impotence sets in as males make a mockery of manhood and become a deadly cartoon version of what they think a man should be.

Leaders in the urban community long ago recognized that the demise of male leadership within the family context coincides with the rise in violence and crime in their neighborhoods.

A boy without a man's imprint is a book without a publisher, a compass without markings, and a code without a cipher.

The wound left by an absent father is one that seeps and bleeds for years.

It also leaves a boy completely unprepared for his duty as a man.

My friend Bart Campolo, who has spent many years doing youth work in the inner city, shared with me this all-too-typical story of a rudderless young man who tried to navigate the swirling waters of manhood:

Bradley grew up in the heart of a Midwest metropolis without a father. His mother and grandmother both were ministers in a small, inner-city storefront church. As a child, Brad was their "golden boy," singing in the little church choir, preaching junior sermons, and being doted on by the largely female members of the congregation.

Even though he was a bit reluctant to break away from this zone of safety, Bradley desperately longed to discover and assert his own masculinity.

Brad started to lift weights, and before long, his physique was huge and imposing. He wrestled at a high level in school competition. At the same time, he began the quiet search for a masculine identity to model. Brad developed close friendships with boys who had fathers and would find excuses to stay at their homes until he was sent home.

Eventually, Brad found his way to the youth group Bart commanded. There, he attached himself to Bart.

All was well until his mother began to sense that her spiritual hold on the boy was slipping away. At that point, she very directly pulled him back into the fold of her little church.

His venture into the world of men was not long enough to train him to be a man. But Brad had made a discovery at Campolo's youth group. Her name was Lila.

Lila, a deeply committed Christian girl, was raised with virtually no parents at all. She deeply longed for a family and a man to love her in a way she had only read about in books and seen in the movies. She believed Brad was that man.

Even though Brad went back to the storefront church run by his mother and grandmother, he continued to see Lila. They were married right out of high school.

Although they were both genuine, loving Christians, within a few years, their marriage was over and Lila was left alone with a baby.

Things had gone wrong almost from the start.

Brad had no idea what to do as a husband or father. It wasn't big stuff like beatings or verbal abuse that doomed the marriage, but rather an accumulation of false expectations.

Brad didn't realize that he needed to come home when he was expected, or at least call when he wasn't going to make it. He didn't know he should help around the house or with the baby. He had no clue that eating meals in front of the TV was not normal family behavior. He didn't know how to listen to his wife's hurts or resolve conflicts. He hadn't learned how to handle money, balance a checkbook, or be responsible with bills. He understood hot, forbidden sex in the context of a dating relationship, but no one had told him what to expect in terms of emotionally connected, married sex. His instincts were way off, especially when the baby came along.

Of course, it didn't help that Lila was similarly unprepared for married life, but as things played out, it became clear that she had a much more realistic idea of her role as a wife than Brad did of his as a husband.

Among the many things Brad had never seen modeled was how to stay with a woman when things got hard.

So he left.

Lila would raise her child alone. Fatherless.

Their baby was a boy.

Perhaps because their segment of society has been so ravaged by the curse of fatherless homes, it has been Christian leaders in the black community who, years ago, pioneered some of the first attempts at developing a meaningful rite of passage for their youth.

Chris McNair, a youth worker in Minneapolis, developed a popular passage program called *Young Lions* for inner-city kids when he realized that the male-saturated beckoning from the streets was stealing his boys before they left middle school.

McNair's focus is on a gritty, overtly male-driven form of youth ministry. And it works.

What's been the norm for fatherless boys in the inner city is quickly becoming the norm in the heartland. Like their urban counterparts, boys in the heartland scurry around the ball fields, sidewalks, and malls of the suburbs, unknowingly but instinctively looking for the model of a man they can etch into their soul.

The imprinter of manhood that every boy seeks comes from one place only: other men.

Men help boys become men. Men set the standards, men challenge the initiates, and men affirm or negate the results.

In spite of what the movies tell us, a woman *never* makes a boy into a man.

A young male may use sex as part of his rite of passage, but it's really the approval of male peers that he's after, not the act itself.

Those men who have been raised with a father or even a father figure can hardly comprehend the incredible vacuum that exists for those boys who aren't. The world of these boys is out of balance. There's a loneliness and longing for some part of the puzzle that the boy can't even define.

Sometimes mothers sense this emptiness in their boys and try to compensate for the void by more mothering, sometimes even smothering. This never works. In fact, it might even create rebellion in the boy. He pushes his mother away in an effort to discover what other boys are naturally given: male influence.

Without male guidance, starvation will set in.

This does not mean that discovering godly manhood is impossible without a man in the picture. It's just much more difficult.

The boy becomes easy prey for male predators, cruelty, gangs, and other dark and twisted offerings presented to fatherless boys. Their pain is masked, because showing it would seem unmanly.

Ironically, while our Christian communities have seemed to notice the plight of the homeless and, in our hospital mode, have created recovery programs for every kind of abuse imaginable, we've done virtually nothing about the empty and hungry young boys we step around each Sunday at church. We have forgotten our biblical mandate to care for the fatherless.

Huge swaths of kids have been functionally abandoned by their fathers (a phone call once in a while and a visit in the summer *does* qualify as functional abandonment) and are in desperate need of the imprint of a real man in their lives.

Godly men can make a difference if we are willing to act.

Donovan first came to our doorstep as a pint-sized pal of one of our own boys.

With a squeaky, high-pitched voice; gleaming teeth crying out for an orthodontist; a sinewy little body; and a disobedient thatch of thick black hair, Donovan became a regular part of the family.

That summer, Donovan was a guest from early morning until late at night. He ate with us, helped with chores, joined us at church and in prayers, and sometimes even received scoldings from us. He returned home only to sleep and, even then, often spent the night at our house.

Through bits and pieces of conversation, Donovan revealed that he had never had a father but that he did know who his father was. Painfully, the boy explained that the man he knew to be his father denied his paternity, and Donovan's mother, for reasons of her own, didn't feel compelled to prove the point by a blood test. "I look just like him," Donovan said with sad resignation.

Since there was no income from the man Donovan's mom had named as the father, his mother worked long hours and the boy went home to an empty house nearly every day.

During those long summer days, it became clear that Donovan needed to be a part of our family much more than our boys needed him as a friend. In fact, it was obvious that what he really relished were those rough touches of manhood he was missing at home.

He was a lousy swimmer. This is not a good thing when you live on an island surrounded by ocean, so I took the boy out into the sea to teach him to swim. Every day I pushed him deeper and farther, always in control but far enough away so that he would take a few gulps of saltwater before I propped him up. "Swim or drown," I said. He swam and felt stronger for it. (I understand that many women don't think much of this teaching method, but it seems to work well for most of us men.)

Each night I would drive Donovan home, reaching out to shake his hand strongly before he got out of the car. Donovan was starving for the grip of a man in his life and, even now, he values what he received from us that summer. A powerful handshake is the first thing we exchange when we see each other.

I know from experience the importance of a strong handshake. The strong handshake of a man and the example behind that extended hand helped pull me through the turbulence of my own fatherless youth.

A godly youth pastor people called Von was the man behind the handshake.

Von's strong handshake was one of his trademarks, as was his impeccable punctuality and his trustworthiness.

He was to me what I had the privilege of being for Donovan: a model of manhood to look up to.

Being the oldest, I had the best shot at our dad during the years he was around. But as I edged toward puberty, he slowly vanished and I was left rudderless at a time of life when one needs all the steering possible.

Naturally, no boy consciously thinks, *I'm missing the imprint of a man in my life.* It's a vague hunger, mixed up and confused with all the other hungers that bud in the late-elementary or middle-school years.

I was fortunate to find myself in the orbit of Von during this time, and he became a surrogate father to me and to the rest of the small herd of high-energy, fatherless boys constantly orbiting around him.

Von was an actual warrior with authentic war stories. He was an adventurer of the Indiana Jones mold, with a wall of blowguns, genuine poisonous darts, wickedly curved scimitars, and a massive collection of huge, exotic, and evil-looking bugs brought back from the jungles of Africa and South America. He had eaten grubs, monkeys, parrots, and other out-of-the-ordinary cuisine and would describe in detail the taste and texture of each to his enthralled and grossed-out audience.

Von would even arrange to take some of us with him on his annual expeditions to newly reached people groups in distant jungles or on his weekly short trips into the bowels of poverty in some Mexican slum.

Von caught rattlesnakes with a stick and his bare hands. He knew how to pull ingenious practical jokes, fix small engines, and rig nonlethal electrical charges to the hubcaps of cars in order to discourage neighborhood dogs from lifting their legs. And he shared his secrets with us.

He taught us to use a stick shift and clutch, to work electronic devices, edit movies, and plenty of other practical bits of knowledge and tasks.

He talked to us frankly about subjects men need to know about: sex, responsibility, integrity, courage, wisdom, and sacrifice. Most importantly of all, he shared with us his mighty, strong, and very masculine image of God.

He imprinted the characteristics of a godly man onto each of us fatherless boys.

Many members of that pack, some with families and boys of our own now, still honor him as one would a father.

I believe that it is the *holy duty* of the church to provide an imprint of manhood for those in our communities who lack an involved man in their lives.

Both the Hebrew society of the Old Testament and those in the New Testament church understood their roles in the lives of children deprived of male leadership. Scripture is laced with a call to care for those who are growing outside the bounds of a "normal" family. Consider:

> He defends the cause of the fatherless and the widow, and loves the alien, giving him food and clothing. (Deuteronomy 10:18)
>
> Do not deprive the alien or the fatherless of justice, or take the cloak of the widow as a pledge. (Deuteronomy 24:17)
>
> He is a Father to the fatherless; he gives justice to the widows, for he is holy. (Psalm 68:5, TLB)
>
> Religion that God our Father accepts as pure and faultless is this: to look after orphans and widows in their distress and to keep oneself from being polluted by the world. (James 1:27)

All too often, the modern church acts as if these fatherless children don't exist, choosing to focus our energy on intact family units with one man and one woman.

Naturally, a young man's own father is the ideal person to teach the boy about the nature of manhood. In recent years, evangelicals in particular have had an increased awareness of the mysterious, God-designed dynamics that take place between a father and a son. Some excellent resources such as Robert Lewis's *Raising a Modern-Day Knight,* the Promise Keepers' *Passage* program, and James Dobson's *Bringing Up Boys* have, in various ways, provided resources and ideas to strengthen and make intentional that imprint.

But in spite of what Christian men are attempting to do for their own sons, the reality is that for a great number of boys, the way to manhood is void of any positive male guidance at all. Males are all around, but few are men. Genetics may turn a boy into a man on the outside, but appearance is all there is. Our boys need men who are men through and through. Even the sons of good Christian fathers still need affirming exposure to other models of Christian manhood.

This is where the church must step in. We must offer a virile, attractive, muscular model of manhood and men with hearts big enough to reach out to even those boys who aren't their own sons.

Here and there a few churches are taking a crack at the problem. In our attempt to stand in the gap for boys on the journey to manhood, my church here in Hawaii, Kauai Christian Fellowship, has created a Christ-centered rite of passage called, "Passed Thru Fire."

This experience allows the men of the church to do the necessary job of setting and modeling the standard of godly manhood, then challenging boys both inside and outside the church walls to step up to those principles in their own lives.

But it will take more than a few of us to turn the tide; it will take the church as a whole to get serious about helping boys reach a real manhood.

I love learning; it was school I hated. I used to cut school to go learn something.

—Eric Jensen

6 TEACHING TO THEIR DISADVANTAGE

The Bible does not mandate Sunday school, yet the Sunday school hour is, outside of the Christian home, the *primary* exposure that most young males in North America have to the concepts of Christianity. For those children who don't come from a Christian home, it's usually the *only* exposure kids have to Christianity. And the mental picture that most boys have of Sunday school, and therefore of Christianity as a whole, is often not very flattering. The Sunday school program is very often weak, boring, irrelevant, and unexciting for boys. It does very little to grab and keep the attention, interest, and involvement of strong young males.

This has not always been the case. Sunday school began as a powerful, courageous movement. Its founders were seen as revolutionaries who took on the culture and the Christian establishment. They fought for a moral principle, for a change in society, and for a cause bigger than themselves. The leaders were dynamic, forceful, and insightful men.

Gloucester, England in the late eighteenth century was similar to other British cities coming to terms with the industrial revolution. In a society that had a clearly delineated class system, the many changes sweeping the nation were disastrous for those at the bottom of the food chain. Villages were emptied and cities overcrowded as the attraction of jobs swept up those hoping for a way out of poverty.

The resulting exodus flooded cities with poor inhabitants beyond the infrastructures' means to handle them. The result? Ever widening slums, rampant disease, and more poverty.

This social upheaval severed, for the most part, the roots of piety and morality that life in the village had once encouraged.

Cheap labor was needed, and every city had an abundance of children employed for a pittance in what we would now call sweatshops.

Child-labor laws being nonexistent, the process quickly developed into a cycle of despair as children, working sixty hours per week or more, were forced to forego any kind of education. As the industrial revolution was being built on the backs of society's weakest members, the social and familial results were disastrous. The poverty vortex that pulled these children in also spun off a wild increase in juvenile crime, plague, and misery.

Robert Raikes (1736–1811) was a newspaper publisher in the city of Gloucester. As a solidly committed Christian, his heart broke for the children of the slums. With the help of an associate, Raikes organized a school for waifs on Sunday from ten in the morning until two in the afternoon with an hour lunch break and a church service after class. The initial curriculum was elementary reading. The text was God's Word. Within a short time, well over a hundred of Gloucester's slum children, ages six to twelve, were enrolled in this revolutionary experiment.

Opposition was swift and vocal. Many in the Christian community howled that Raikes was violating and desecrating the Sabbath day. But bolstered by an immediate drop in juvenile crime, Robert Raikes and his friends continued their activities and spread the word of this experiment's success.

Before long, the Sunday school movement exploded, as the church led the charge against the exploitation of children. The community of faith was doing something daring and exciting to reach kids for Christ while working to improve their temporal lives.

Sunday school started as a gutsy, bold endeavor. Those adjectives probably would not be used to describe our current Sunday-morning classes.

Both inside and outside the church, Sunday school has earned the reputation of being "dorky." Regardless of whether or not this is an accurate description, it means that we're often starting behind the curve when it comes to attracting kids from outside the church family.

Small pluses or minuses can tip the scale toward a class attracting boys or repelling them. Let's consider some potential assets and liabilities that can result in the church either drawing in and keeping boys or sending them away.

AUTHORITY

There is no easy way to say this: Male teachers generally have more authority in the mind of boys than do female teachers. It has nothing to do with brilliance, care, devotion, or preparedness. It has everything to do with the "macho" factor. An adult male is considered dangerous to the average young buck. Unlike the female, the male is—in the boy's mind—far more unpredictable and powerful. And boys honor power and cruelly exploit weakness. Just watch them on the playing field.

Many boys tend to view women in authority as extensions of their mothers. They have a sense of how an adult woman will think and react based upon the way their mothers think and react.

But men, on the other hand, are somewhat of a mystery. Men often ignore little boys—or at least they *seem* to ignore them, compared to the attention female adults lavish upon them. Men don't hand out compassion and sympathy as quickly as women tend to do over the skinned knee, the knot on the head, or the dead bird. A young boy is more likely to hear, "It serves you right for going too fast down the hill!" or "Come on, be tough! Don't cry over a little road rash!" from the adult males in his life. The male child loves the tenderness of his mother, but he *craves* the strength of his father.

For male children who live in fatherless households, men are even more heavily shrouded in mystery and power.

The response young boys have to women in authority is often uniquely different from their response to men in authority.

I know this firsthand.

In my seventh-grade year, I somehow missed the deadline for getting into what I felt was the domain of boys: wood shop. Apparently the number of boys applying for shop classes outweighed the ability of the school to service them. They had to do something with the leftovers, and so I, along with a ragtag group of other misfits, was relegated to the dumping ground of guys without shop: boys' choir. It was a choice I neither desired nor cared about nor had any skill in. It was to be a miserable, yearlong state of limbo for the forty complaining boys stuck in the class, but it proved to be a year of pure hell for the teacher whose unfortunate lot in life had cast her into this group of pint-sized anarchists!

The teacher was an older woman, and just by virtue of age and experience she must have had a premonition as to what was coming. Her name was Mrs. Hutton. We, the unwilling subjects, quickly discovered that when the class was incorrigible, which was quite often, Mrs. Hutton would go rapidly from hysterics to tears—tears not of sorrow but of sheer frustration, followed by a quick exit out the side door. This left the lunatics free to run the asylum for as long as it took her to compose herself and return to the fray! It quickly became the intentional goal for many of the more unconscionable boys among us to bring her to this point at least several times a week.

She was supposed to be the authority, but she was not. She was weak; we (as a collective group) were strong. We had no negative emotions about the torment meted out. It seemed just deserts for those who had been shanghaied into boys' choir.

Of course there were (and thankfully still are) female teachers who could strike a degree of terror into any punk seventh grader, but even the worst punishment of the most ferocious woman teacher seemed a mere mosquito bite compared to the discipline a tough male teacher could dish out.

The kind of shenanigans that sent poor Mrs. Hutton to an early retirement would have never gotten off the ground with most male teachers. There is a difference. You can't always define it or explain it, but it has to do with authority. The *maleness* of the teacher endows him with authority that a female rarely elicits in kind.

One crucial key to keeping young boys involved in the church is the active participation of men, particularly in the role of teaching and leading groups. We need men deeply involved in the lives of boys as teachers, leaders, and guides. We need to actively recruit male teachers and, whenever possible, break the classes up into boys and girls with men leading the boys. Men can demand and get more respect from the tougher kids. Men carry with them the natural authority that boys need.

Those working in early childhood education have pointed out that when men are involved in the classroom, even the nature of play changes.

Paul Learned of Standard Publishing comments on what he has observed during his long tenure in children's Sunday school classes: "Women tend to teach the Bible story with pictures, flannel graph, etc., while men simulate the story so children can experience the storm on Lake Galilee with blue tarps for the lake, a cardboard box for the boat, a fan for the wind, and mist bottles sprayed into a fan for the rain. Men are much more physical, more realistic, more experiential in their teaching methods."

The predominance of female teachers and group leaders in places where young boys are involved often serves as a minus rather than a plus in the large scope of things.

And this is *not* the women's fault.

Women often teach because women love children. Women often teach because it is presumed (by men) that it's their task to fulfill. And women sometimes teach out of raw guilt.

Christian men *must* step up to the plate. The payoff for teaching a squirrelly bunch of fourth-graders may not seem as rewarding as the payoff for leading an adult study, but the results actually may be more profound for the kingdom of God. (It was a male Sunday school teacher who had the greatest impact on evangelist Dwight L. Moody.)

The promises that follow Christ's teaching on being faithful *in* little (Matthew 25:21) might come to us as a result of being faithful *to those who are* little.

MALE-APPROPRIATE TEACHING MATERIAL

If you take the time to check out the children's curriculum used in today's churches, you'll notice that a fair portion of it is written and created by women. Although some publishers have male editors, often their primary role is to check for theological content, not necessarily specific applicability for young boys.

I know this for a fact through my experience as director of youth curriculum development for a major Christian publishing house.

Don't misunderstand me. There's some really good stuff in much of the material currently on the market, and by and large, editors and writers do a decent job. But woven into a lot of the materials are ideas that are quite clearly from the perspective of a woman, which is as it should be, coming from a woman writer.

And that stuff is pretty wonderful . . . for girls. But it often leaves something to be desired when it comes to connecting with the minds and lives of young guys.

For example, I once read a proposed sixth-grade Sunday school lesson about the parable of the Good Samaritan that clearly illustrates how even the material we use to teach our boys can unintentionally alienate them.

The kickoff activity asked the students to consider "what color they would feel" if they saw a particular tragic incident: a hurt animal or a car accident, for example. What this female curriculum writer obviously didn't realize is that most boys are not likely to "feel" any color whatsoever. The whole idea of "feeling a color" for a young boy, or any boy for that matter, is nonsensical.

Girls may feel colors. Boys, particularly those who are tilting the masculine scale, do not. With activities like this, the lesson gets lost right from the starting block.

Further into the parable, the writer points to examples that, while accurate, probably ring far more true to the mind of a sixth-grade girl than a sixth-grade boy. We learn that the Samaritan displayed compassion, tenderness, and mercy. This is true. But it's also true that for a young male mind dogged for manhood and pushing away anything that has even a hint of the feminine, compassion, tenderness, and mercy are perceived of as *female* traits.

During this period of life, a boy will often jettison ideas that he perceives as feminine since they don't connect with the model of masculinity he aspires to imitate.

Of course, the parable offers some firm examples that any testosterone-plagued young man can identify with. Courage, protection, responsibility—all can be found in the story. By leading with these traits, we can introduce mercy and compassion as well. But when we lead with mercy and compassion, we hit the Off switch in the little male mind before the lesson can be absorbed.

The problem is that because women often create the materials we use to teach our boys, the concepts and teaching activities used are (understandably) put through a female filter and, in the end, appeal mostly to girls. Women teachers usually don't see this distinction because the lesson likely rings true to their worldview.

This dilemma is true for much of life. Women see things through the eyes of their womanhood, men through the eyes of their manhood . . . even things in the Bible.

The solution here is to be aware of what we are teaching and encourage tinkering with materials to make them more applicable to the target audience, male or female. Those who teach boys should be advised to comb through curriculum, to recreate activities that don't fly with male perceptions, and to possibly even change the emphasis of a lesson plan to work with boys. Ditto for those teaching girls, by the way.

Also, publishing houses appreciate helpful feedback. If a teacher finds that the material is missing the mark with boys on a regular basis, curriculum developers need to know this in order to improve the material.

ACTIVE VERSUS PASSIVE LEARNING

Another element conspiring against young boys in the church is the idea that noise, activity, and action (otherwise known as rowdiness) are not welcome at church. Quietness, industry, reverence, and passivity are rewarded. Kids (almost always boys) who act up, get bored, or create disturbances quickly get the message that they're not desirable. And who wants to stay where you're not wanted?

We must remember that it's God himself who created our personalities. It's his design that tells us when to get up and move, his prodding that motivates us toward action and engagement, his model that is put off by passivity and longs for excitement. The "shut up, sit down, be quiet, and listen" mentality of teaching works against what God himself has created.

Yet rare is the classroom that works to accommodate the wiggling, noisy, energetic boy.

What works with boys isn't all that hard to figure out. Boys like to *do* things, not just to talk about things. Boys want to move, to act out, and to create. This may mean that the walls of the classroom are just starting points for the group. It may mean there needs to be lots of mobility, activity, and possibly even messing up those nicely starched clothes Mom sent them off to church in. It might involve competition and contests. It might include worms and fishing poles, mud and muck. Whatever it is, most girls would probably hate it.

There are solutions. When implemented, these solutions can tilt the scale in the direction of drawing boys into the community of Christ. These solutions must be undertaken in concert with other branches of the church; otherwise we may gain strong boys only to lose them a few years later by the mishandling of some other department.

A quick and simple solution is to *separate boys and girls,* even if there are only two or three boys. Put the apples in one place and the oranges in another. In tandem with this solution is to make sure that there is a *male teacher* for the boys (yes, easier said than done). Boys will respond best to a teacher whose physical presence and personality demand respect. Since their authority is already vested in what they do, police officers, firefighters, and construction workers, for example, make ideal teachers for young boys.

In addition, we must encourage teachers to *consider the strong males in the class as the common denominator* in the group. The teacher should check his teaching materials for appropriateness by asking himself, *Would* ________ (fill in the blank with the rowdiest boy in your group) *relate to this or do this activity?* Teachers should feel free to change or edit the material to best fit the kids.

Our teachers need the freedom to *break out of the box.* Do things with your boys that are active and full of vigor. Activities are not the opposite of teaching; indeed, lots of great teaching can occur in the midst of noise and energy. Leave the site. Do things. Make things. Allow your students to grasp, feel, and move as part of the lesson plan.

Toss the watch and judge how long the lessons should be by the active involvement of the boys. When they've had enough, go out and play ball.

I've listed below a few samples of activities that have a high success rate with young boys.

- **SHOOT A VIDEO.** Rather than just telling the parable of the Good Samaritan, why not act it out with plenty of pummeling and ketchup? Rolls of toilet paper can double as bandages. Making the movie is only half the fun. Be sure you show it, along with a full complement of popcorn and soda.

- **GO ON LOCATION.** Take your class to a construction site to talk about Christ as our foundation or to the cemetery to talk about the raising of Lazarus. Gross them out at a pig farm when you teach the lesson of the Prodigal Son. Head to the fishpond with bait and poles to talk about being fishers of men.

- **MAKE SOMETHING.** Bring them to your workshop or garage and create tie-ins to the lesson using saw, wood, nails, and glue.

- **BE A BUG COLLECTOR.** Send everyone out with a jar and a magnifying glass to collect examples of God's creative handiwork in the bug world.

- **GET DIRTY.** Drag out plaster of paris and foam blocks, and carve up and plaster your own version of the temple based on drawings. Then lessons that take place in the temple—such as Jesus chasing out the money changers—will become more real to your boys.

CREATE MALE-ORIENTED PROGRAMS, ACTIVITIES, OR EVENTS

If the Sunday school program is too cumbersome to change in order to meet the needs of boys, you can still grab the attention of young males using creative alternatives.

Consider starting an all-boy program or club in your church. These groups tend to be very attractive to boys, full of male leadership, and helpful in projecting an image of the Christian faith that's palatable to males.

"Guys only" camping trips or fishing trips are especially attractive to boys because they get to be outside, and men usually lead these trips.

Because boys learn about Christian manhood from watching and listening to Christian men, it's during these guy-oriented activities that the real communication of God's love takes place. Every effort should be made to involve the boys of the church and their friends in these kinds of activities.

Naturally, making young, active males the common denominator will not please everyone. Some will consider this to be an off-balance or unnecessary focus. Some will see it as chauvinistic, even hostile to women.

By emphasizing boy-oriented activities, a church youth group is able to balance out the gender count and create a male environment: otherwise, the group tends to drift toward greater numbers of girls. It's a way to establish a solid equilibrium and make the church attractive to both boys and girls.

The fact remains that boys are usually better led, better taught, and better communicated to by men. And it's this vital age group (between the fourth and ninth grades) that most needs the help and involvement of strong Christian men.

For us, with the rule of right and wrong given by Christ, there is nothing for which we have no standard. And there is no greatness where there is not simplicity, goodness and truth.

—Leo Tolstoy
War and Peace

7 HOW A MAN IS MADE

Men don't just appear. They are made, carved, and molded by the older men who have influence in their lives and by the culture they wish to be accepted by.

Throughout history, the honor of being a guardian of a culture's spiritual values, core beliefs, and standards of behavior was bestowed upon a boy who had successfully gone through some kind of rite, test, or ordeal.

In cultures that see the need to endow their children with the authority of adulthood, one common thread is this: The boy acting alone cannot achieve it. He must have the help and approval of other men in order to enter into real manhood.

Apart from initiation, which we'll talk about in chapter 9, there are a number of common elements that go into the making of a man.

A MAN IS MADE BY HONORING WISDOM AND EXPERIENCE

Western culture has turned youth into a frightening cult. Baby boomers, now on the downward slope of our culture's definition of beauty and virility, are fighting with all their considerable resources to hang on to the look and feel of youth. But the only hope a plastic surgeon, a dose of Viagra, or a fitness routine can offer is a temporary reprieve from the inevitable.

Adolescence—or being a "pre-warrior," as Robert Bly calls it in *Iron John*—is no longer an awkward period of life that you must get through as quickly as possible. It's now a state of life in which to live for as long as possible.

Youth is adored and worshiped; old age is ignored, fought against, abhorred. Our culture has little or no place for those who are the elders of society.

The role of an elder is a respected idea in Scripture. It is conferred on someone who is not just an ecclesiastical leader, such as the men who governed the ancient Christian churches, but who has the whiteness of time upon his head and is considered to be a receptacle of wisdom and a person of honor.

The Bible tells us that "white hair is a crown of glory and is seen most among the godly" (Proverbs 16:31, TLB).

While there do seem to be some hopeful stirrings of this notion—such as the long overdue honor and recognition being given for the sacrifices of the eldest members of our society, what Tom Brokaw calls "the Greatest Generation"—the cult of youth still reigns supreme.

The typical young man who has spent little face-to-face time with any elder other than a relative has little sense of the depths of good judgment, understanding, and acumen stored within the ancient mind. The only way for boys and young men to appreciate the wisdom, experience, and sacrifice of their elders is through exposure. And the best kind of exposure is found in stories.

During our church's first *Passed Thru Fire* weekend event, we included a time for the men to tell their stories to the boys. This was done more as an impulse, a "seemed like a good idea at the time" notion. I was a little afraid that men might balk at giving everyone a glimpse of their souls and that the results would be flat—or worse, condescending. I had no idea the incredible power these "man stories" would unleash.

The men came up one at a time. They sat on a tall stool in front of the boys and told stories, *their* stories, simple and unrehearsed. They didn't preach or attempt to teach or instruct. In five or ten minutes, they exposed, sometimes painfully and always candidly, a slice of their life that they thought would be helpful, interesting, or relevant to young boys on a quest for manhood.

Some of the stories were hair-raising.

Bob, a laconic, affable real estate agent told of how the twelve-seater twin prop he and eight others had chartered for a fishing trip ran out of gas in midair and crash-landed in a thick forest . . . without one fatality.

Doug, a pharmacist, pulled up his shirt and showed the entry and exit bullet wounds he received during a robbery in which he was shot and his boss was killed.

As one might imagine, not a boy moved an inch during those stories.

But just as powerful were the simple stories—stories of jobs won or lost, stories of fathers whose deeds were heralded or fathers who were painfully missing in action. Stories about struggles, women, work, courage, and lack of courage. Stories about success and failure.

Many of the boys knew the men who were telling these stories from church. Before, they had been just nameless old guys. Suddenly they were men with dimension, experience, and wisdom born of time and struggle. They had rolled up their sleeves and shown their war wounds. And they were respected for it.

Creating an opportunity for stories builds respect and reverence for those of hoary head.

Because of our child-centered culture and the lack of understanding and honor for the aged, it's important for a church to take direct and intentional steps in order to reintroduce this kind of respect into their children's lives.

Simple rules of conduct can be implemented. For example, age should be given priority. Rather than allowing hordes of hungry youngsters to race to the front of the line at a church potluck, a rule could be made that says the line will always start with the oldest and work backwards. Age has priority.

So what if the pizza is gone when the kids get there? It should be considered a tribute to the dues these wise folks have paid if they get the first and the best!

Boys don't come to this understanding by themselves. They must be taught.

A MAN IS MADE THROUGH THE COMPANY OF MEN

While fathers are critical to the shaping of a boy into a man, they aren't sufficient. A father should not be seen as independent from the community of men. His involvement is crucial not only in the imprint stage of a boy's development, but also at the time he introduces the boy to the larger male community. The father brings forth his son, the candidate, and other men join him in the process of initiation.

Small glimpses of this process can be seen played out in everyday life.

A father takes his son fishing. He teaches him how to tie the lure, cast the line, and glide the pole. He shows him the secret places where the fish lurk; he schools him in the rules of the hunt. And then he hands the pole over to the boy.

If the boy has learned well, if he's lucky enough to have the fish strike and deftly handles the pole, he'll have a wiggling trophy to display.

But the real fulfillment of the experience comes when the father meets his adult friends and, with an elegantly simple commendation, pronounces that "the boy learned well; he pulled in a big one today." The other men nod in knowing approval. "Welcome to the club of real fishermen," they say, their understated encouragement taking the form of admiration, a low whistle, or a hearty pat on the back.

The boy has been instructed, guided, and imprinted in the art of fishing by his father. The boy proves himself and is then presented to the larger community of men for its approval. When he gets home, women and siblings will honor him as well. He has become a genuine "fisher*man*."

It is this interplay, this connectedness with not only the father but with the men of the community as well, that brings a boy into the fold of men.

A boy on his journey to manhood must not only leave the protective custody of his mother, but he must someday make a break from his father as well. He must become his own man. This is difficult to do alone. The "tribe" of men must be a part of the process in order to give validity to the passage.

This gathering of the male ranks to confer manhood upon a boy is the missing piece in our current culture. Even in our churches, it's the blank page in the continuum from boyhood to manhood.

Once a boy has crossed into manhood, it's the company of men that must present him in this new role to society and even to his parents.

In ancient cultures, elaborate ceremonies took place to present the successful inductee, now endowed with the privileges of manhood, back to the tribe.

Only men can present this gift to a boy. Women are neither on the playing field nor the team. And the boy cannot do it by himself. It must come from a company of men.

A MAN IS MADE THROUGH DOSES OF LOVING BRUTALITY

Men are made not by the soft gloves of comfort but by coming face-to-face with raw and often ugly brutality. Every boot camp in the world is built on this principle; every serious playing field encourages it.

Boys know this instinctively and practice various forms of brutality toward each other: shunning, rejecting, taunting, pushing, fighting, and competing. They gloat in their victories and heartlessly rest their feet upon the corpses of their victims.

Lacking the visible, God-directed standard that would prevent it, boys often visit their brutality on the weakest member of the group, tearing into his soul and creating wounds he will remember for a lifetime. It is precisely God's standards that step in to offer protection, care, and encouragement to the physically or socially inept (see Luke 14:12-14).

But there is a kind of stark preparedness that must be visited upon a boy in order to equip him for the journey into manhood.

I call it loving brutality. It comes from men.

Women coddle. Women shield. Women often have a difficult time imagining their sons being anything other than charming, tousle-headed children nestled upon their breasts.

Men know that they must take a boy and dirty him. They must make him hard, tough, and callous. They must forbid him to acknowledge his pain—they muffle his cry, they steel his determination. This is not abuse. It's life preparation, the building of his discipline, the mastering of his fear, and the controlling of his emotions. They know that he must develop this grit in order to survive in the workplace, playing field, or battlefield. They know that in spite of what women *say* they are looking for in a man, there will be little respect for a weak, timid, fearful, or cowardly man. The boy must learn that there is truth in the cliché that instructs him to hold his damaged guts in and drag himself through the fight for as long as he is able.

Men know the danger this can breed. Without a moral compass, viciousness sets in. This is why they must teach boys about honor, fair play, and justice. Men know that there will come a day, after a boy has learned to be hard, when he must learn once again to soften and to acknowledge and embrace pain. Men know that the danger of developing the ability to be hard is to block all the emotional exits permanently and become sullen and tormented.

Men understand a boy's desire to be safe, nurtured, and accepted.

But boys who want to be men must know how to properly handle rejection, because they will probably get a lot of it, especially when they start to notice girls.

Since boys are the ones who do most of the initiating in male/female relationships, they are usually the first to feel the consequences of direct rejection. (Girls must deal with rejection as well, but it's usually the passive "not being chosen" form.) To be outright rejected by a girl he admires cuts to the core of a boy's personality and accentuates his helplessness. The reaction of many boys is to try harder, become more powerful (because boys sense that girls have a high regard for power), or simply turn women into objects. To be hurt by an object causes far less pain than to be hurt by a person.

Men know that a boy must face rejection over and over . . . and must learn to deal with it appropriately.

Men know the nest will become a dangerous place if a boy stays there too long, so he must be hurled out. He must risk disaster and be forced to fly.

Consider this real-life situation: A boy finds himself on a camp out. During the process of gathering wood he gets a sliver in his hand. He races back to the camp, whimpering and crying. Adults move toward him. He holds out his palm and moans his complaint. The eyes of the men glance at the wound. They assess its severity. They judge the boy's toughness . . . and if he's found wanting, the boy senses that the body language of the men condemns him. Their eyes break contact; they step back from the boy and turn in disgust, slightly shaking their heads in revulsion for his weakness as a woman rushes to console and aid. It's a brutal message, subtly delivered: *You're not a man in our eyes.*

If the boy forgets his sleeping bag (one of his few responsibilities to remember for the camping trip), it's usually a man who suggests that the boy "learn his lesson" by shivering the night away wrapped in all the clothes he brought.

It's a principle not foreign to Scripture: "No discipline seems pleasant at the time, but painful. Later on, however, it produces a harvest of righteousness and peace for those who have been trained by it" (Hebrews 12:11).

This is loving brutality.

The very idea may cause some to bristle in horror. It may seem a fallback to the primitive, outdated thinking that created a guts-and-glory standard of manhood that's both unrealistic and hurtful to men and women.

But the balance is not found in redesigning ourselves into new, sensitive men. It's found in embracing strength and limitations, courage and fear, steeliness and vulnerability. Take a look at the first words in each of these couplets. For a boy emerging from the safety of his childhood, these are the words that must be impressed upon him.

It's the role of men to enforce the principles that say, "We reap what we sow," "We get what we work for," and "We must pay the piper." It's the role of men to see to it that our boys "learn the hard way." While these are universal truths, they make a strong impression in a man's world as he sees himself as the first line of responsibility for reaping, sowing, laboring, and paying. And adult men use these coded expressions that make perfect sense to them in order to tell the boys, "Whatever doesn't kill you makes you stronger."

MEN ARE MADE THROUGH LOYALTY TO A STANDARD

In the battles men have fought, even through the American Civil War, men gathered around, identified with, and honored a company standard. Even in biblical times, a standard was used in warfare (see Jeremiah 4:21).

This standard, or flag, typically represented the community from which the warriors came. In times past, the women of the town usually made the flag and presented it to the soldiers with great love and solemn ceremony. The man who carried it was considered to have great honor and bravery, for he often led the way into battle, unarmed and clutching the company standard as the focal point of the charging men.

Holding the standard aloft was a dangerous task. The bearer served as the representative of his company and, as such, was the first one at whom the enemy would take aim. The mortality rate was extremely high for standard bearers.

We men no longer charge into war with our battle-stained standards leading the way, but that doesn't mean that what the standard represents has vanished. The standard held aloft in the past is much the same as the moral standards of today.

All men have a set of standards by which they measure the manhood of a fellow male. Many times these standards have a universal sweep, such as the honor of courage or the disgrace of cowardice. Sometimes the standards become a twisted mockery of what men know in their soul to be the genuine marks of a man, such as the thuggery and brutal demeaning of women that typifies the music and verbiage of gang members or gang wanna-bes.

For a boy struggling toward manhood, God-breathed standards of masculinity must be the banners that true men rally behind and look to for guidance and inspiration. Those standards should be raised high and celebrated. They should define our masculinity and give measure to our manhood.

What are colors men, particularly men of God, gather behind? Here is a short list of some of the most prominent. As we shall see in a later chapter, these are the standards that we can offer to our boys as the supreme model of manhood. A man in the image of God cannot be made without them.

RIGHTEOUSNESS

In simple terms, this means right standing before God and man. The Bible clearly teaches that righteousness is not something humans can create on our own. We can only be righteous in the eyes of God if we trust in the sacrifice Christ made on the cross for our sins and failures.

The new life instilled in each believer and the power of the Holy Spirit then gives us the ability and insight to live in an honorable way with our fellow human beings.

Righteousness starts with understanding who God is and who we are . . . and who we are not. Proverbs tells us, "The reverence and fear of God are basic to all wisdom" (Proverbs 9:10, TLB). This trait is the cornerstone of wisdom. It's the true north on the compass that makes all the other markings on the compass make sense.

Righteousness then spreads to our connectedness to God and our willingness to live by his design and precepts. "But seek first his kingdom and his righteousness" (Matthew 6:33).

Righteousness is the very thing that makes all of the important attributes of manhood actually attainable. We don't become men by our own steam and energy, but by the strength of God working through us.

COURAGE

Courage comes in many forms. Often we think of it as some kind of heroic bravery, but courage can also be quiet and unseen. Courage can demand that we risk our lives or courage can demand that we risk our popularity. Courage isn't recklessness—that's merely foolishness married to bravado. Courage may demand strong sacrifice, but it is always driven by an honorable reason.

Courage is illustrated throughout the Bible. Moses pushed Joshua to be courageous in front of the whole nation of Israel (Deuteronomy 3:21-22). King David gave Solomon a wonderful pep talk about strength and courage (1 Chronicles 28:20). Paul extols the guys in the

Corinthian church to "keep your eyes open for spiritual danger; stand true to the Lord; act like men; be strong" (1 Corinthians 16:13, TLB).

Courage is part of the fiber it takes to be a man.

INTEGRITY

This is an overarching word that covers a multitude of areas. It means that we have common honesty, that our word is true. It means we stand behind our craftsmanship and it means we don't take improper shortcuts or cheat where we can get away with it. It means we act with honor even if others don't. Integrity spills over into the workplace, the sports field, and the home. Integrity demands that we speak the truth even if the truth is not in our favor. Scripture is big on integrity issues. Integrity is an essential part of the character of manhood. Integrity was the condition of leadership among the Hebrews as well as the early church (see Exodus 18:21 and Titus 1:7). It was necessary for true worship (see Psalm 15:1-5). It allowed for security of heart and soul (Proverbs 10:9). It was determined by faithfulness in small things as well as things of great importance (Luke 16:10).

Integrity is the indispensable factor in a wedding vow. The fact that so many of those vows are broken is a sad commentary on how little integrity is woven into the men (and women) of our modern culture.

Integrity is a trait that, if violated, demeans our claim to manhood.

CARE AND PROTECTION FOR THE WEAK AND UNLOVELY

The call of a man is the call to be a protector. Protecting the family almost comes naturally for men, but the demand goes much farther. It's a commitment to stand up for, care for, and protect society's weakest and saddest members. History shows that those men who use the weak as their victims end up as monsters, and those men who protect and care for the "least of these" end up as something great—not only in the eyes of their peers, but in the eyes of God.

The duty of a man of God is to help carry those who, through no fault of their own, are weak. Notice the sensibility that rings true in Paul's counsel to the Thessalonian church: "Dear brothers, warn those who are lazy, comfort those who are frightened, take tender care of those who are weak, and be patient with everyone" (1 Thessalonians 5:14). Shirkers get booted on the side of the head, but the genuinely needy are cared for with tenderness.

The heart to care for the unlovely is a vital quality for a man to develop. Every church, every youth group, ought to be a safe and supportive place for the "rejects" of the world. Weak and broken bodies often house blazing spirits. Those whose minds seem hopelessly simple or mentally handicapped may very well be those "angels among us."

When the fragile are cared for, it's a sign of strength. The feeble should be able to find a safe place in the company of men.

SELF-CONTROL

Most males have strong physical appetites. The modern culture has given up resisting those demands of the flesh and, instead, counsels surrender. A real man understands that it is important to control and sometimes deny the satisfaction of the flesh. Of course, self-control spills over into other areas as well. By getting a handle on speech, temper, and other areas that require self-discipline, a boy will grow into a man that others respect and admire.

The apostle Peter was not always the best model of self-control. His tendency to engage his gums far ahead of his brain is obvious in the Gospels. But Peter was a learner. And because he learned, he was able to counsel with authority in his second letter to the churches:

> For this very reason, make every effort to add to your faith goodness; and to goodness, knowledge; and to knowledge, self-control; and to self-control, perseverance; and to perseverance, godliness. (2 Peter 1:5-6)

Self-control is a product the Holy Spirit brings to a life lived in close connection with God (see Galatians 5:22). It's not something that appears magically. Rather, it's connected with godly choices and personal discipline.

RESPONSIBILITY

"Carry your own weight." "Do your duty." "Take responsibility for your actions." "The buck stops here." These are words men speak with intense ownership.

Personal responsibility is the scary and essential step into manhood that a young man needs to feel right down to the bone.

I remember when I was told, "You're gonna need to carry your own weight now." I was a junior in high school and money was tight at home. I had four younger siblings who needed to be cared for. I was old enough to care for myself, which meant old enough to get a job and go to school at the same time. I worked a forty-hour week through the rest of my school days.

I didn't know it at the time, but "carrying my own weight" was a responsibility straight out of Scripture: "For each one should carry his own load" (Galatians 6:5).

A godly man is responsible for providing for his family: "If anyone does not provide for his relatives, and especially for his immediate family, he has denied the faith and is worse than an unbeliever" (1 Timothy 5:8).

Peter and Paul both give men the responsibility to love and care for their wives (1 Peter 3:7; Ephesians 5:25). Men are also required to train and instruct their children in things of God (Ephesians 6:4).

Real men have a biblical responsibility to work for a living and not live off the sweat of others. "Even while we were still there with you, we gave you this rule: 'He who does not work shall not eat' " (2 Thessalonians 3:10, TLB). Even today, several thousand years after those words were written, a freeloading male draws disgust from other men.

The Bible instructs men to invest their labor in something useful enough that it will allow them to care for themselves, their families, and others in the community of faith who are in need (see 1 Thessalonians 4:11).

And unlike modern culture, where victims are plentiful, the Bible refuses to let men wiggle away from taking responsibility for their actions (see 1 Corinthians 3:13-15).

True men of God, men of responsibility, help boys understand the awesome duties that come with the title of "man."

A MAN IS MADE BY LETTING GO OF CHILDHOOD

It's like this: "When I was a child I spoke and thought and reasoned as a child does. But when I became a man my thoughts grew far beyond those of my childhood, and now I have put away the childish things" (1 Corinthians 13:11, TLB).

Most of the ancient rites of passage made a clear delineation between childhood and adulthood. There comes a time when we all must leave the comforts of childhood and carry the burdens of being adults.

In a culture that encourages young people to act as adults in some areas (sexual behavior, birth control, personal use of wealth) but at the same time celebrates irresponsibility and childish thinking, the understanding of what it means to leave childhood behind is muddy for many teens.

Leaving childhood means learning the skills and duties of adulthood. It means becoming a giver rather than a taker.

Adult mentors can have a strong influence by acting as guides for boys who desire to be men. Instruction as to what is expected from them as men is far preferable to allowing a boy to figure it out on his own. Men need to challenge the maturity of youth who are pretending to be men.

When they model attributes of manhood, men of the church can be the conduits for moving boys into manhood by giving them an understanding of and commitment to the things that really count.

I believe that boys do know that manhood comes with a cost and most are willing, even anxious, to accept the challenge of being a man. We just need to give them the opportunity to do so.

One father is more than a hundred schoolmasters.

–George Herbert

8 HELP FOR DISTANT DADS AND SINGLE MOMS

This chapter is specifically designed for single parents. But even if you're not a single parent, I would encourage you to read through these pages so that you might better understand the struggles and unique needs that come about when a home designed for a pair of parents is reduced to one.

I know it's hard to be a single parent.

Whatever the circumstances that result in single parenthood or occasional custody, this way of life creates an unnatural, wobbly, something-is-missing kind of life for both parent and child. And sometimes it's just plain tough . . . and painful as well.

Just spend a little time with men whose destiny it is to raise their children on weekends, alternate weeks, or in arbitrarily created spots carved out of summer vacation, and you'll almost always find a sense of hopelessness and despair. They have "visitation" rights. Kind of like prisoners or criminals. They sometimes feel like criminals.

If the disintegration of the family was not his choice, a man is often bitter when he considers the fact that he's been forcibly denied the opportunity to truly father.

Men like this know that the idea of "quality time" is used as a placebo to calm the angst of those who don't have daily access to their children. They understand deep in their souls that quality time can't be conjured up on a weekend visit; it only comes as a result of vast amounts of *quantity* time. And quantity time is exactly what single fathers are lacking.

For many men, the frustration, emotional turmoil, and disappointment (especially when the child decides that some other option is more inviting than spending the weekend with Dad) are more than they can handle. So they withdraw.

Sometimes they attempt to erase the memory of those children by plunging deeper into business, creating a new family, or returning to an adolescent glut of sex, substances, and stored-up stuff.

They may attempt to get even with the child's mother by withholding or controlling support payments, the only power they have left in parenting. They often become more than distant. Sometimes they vanish.

Children sense this abandonment. They have no concept of the forces and emotions driving it. All they know is that they are a part of that group of unlucky children who have no father. Sometimes they find a surrogate. Sometimes they react with fierce anger, and sometimes they cap off that anger only to see it bubble over later in life.

Women, too, struggle with singleness, especially when it comes to raising sons.

The world of mother and son is complicated by the fact that the boy often takes on the role of "man of the house" when, in fact, God has created him to be only a "boy in the house."

A hurting mother sometimes turns to her son for emotional support or solace—support and solace that a boy may not be able to or should not have to give.

If finances are tight, it's usually the boy who must get a job to help the family.

When my father vanished and finances became uncertain, my mother told me if I wanted anything in this world I would have to get a real job. So I did. Forty hours a week. I was a junior in high school. The money I made went to keep me in food, clothing, and entertainment. I left school at noon every day and came home at ten-thirty every night. If I were motivated at that time of night, I would start on some homework. I was seldom motivated.

This created a family condition similar to an out-of-balance washing machine. There was lots of noise and banging about as my mother attempted to be an authority figure for an eleventh grader, while I insisted that I had the right to liberty, purchased at the cost of working a forty-hour week *and* going to school.

As the mind of a boy slowly transforms into the mind of a man, a mother may find herself unable to understand the metamorphosis.

In the midst of increasing confrontation, she may lose the ability to discipline and may give up trying.

If she works outside the home, supervision and accountability issues become thorny as a boy begins to feel his independence.

Sometimes a woman sees that her son is moving beyond her control and she understands that he needs a father. If that father is available, the mother even wonders if her son should move in with him. But conflicts over the quality of parenting (her lifestyle or his) and her fear of prematurely losing the child from the home—or even worse, the fear of losing his affection and being rejected by the boy if she does let him move out—creates a crisis of the heart.

Finally, there's the dread that perhaps her boy will somehow grow up stilted, never knowing how to be a father or a husband because there's no father or husband to model those skills.

The absence of a father creates a vacuum that a mother cannot hope to fill. Only a man can fill it.

This is a hard concept for many single mothers to grasp, even when they're nodding their heads in agreement.

Fathers tend to be rough-and-tumble. They're usually physical with their children, especially their boys. This is unintentional training for the world of men.

From my experience, I've found that men tend to treat the whole process of growing up differently than do women. Women, by nature, move quickly towards nurturing. Men, for the most part, have no idea what that word means. In fact, even if men can figure out what it means to nurture, they usually can't see any reason to do *that* to a boy, as it will obviously keep him from growing into manhood.

Most men think you need to make a boy tough in order to face the challenges of the world—and this won't come by coddling him.

You can see these two natures in operation if you listen to a typical family exchange:

Junior is crawling up a tree.

Mom: "Be careful, dear; don't go any farther."

Dad: "See if you can touch that orange colored leaf. Yeah, that one up there, ten feet more."

Junior comes in with a case of road rash on his knee.

Mom: "Oh, my poor baby, does it hurt? Let me fix it."

Dad: "You're not going to cry over that little scratch, are you?"

Junior complains he's getting picked on in school.

Mom: "Who is picking on you? I'll call the school and talk to the principal."

Dad: "If he hits you, you have my permission to sock him right back!"

Junior comes in with a slug.

Mom: "GET THAT THING OUT OF HERE!"
Dad: "Hey, have you ever seen what happens when you put salt on these things?"

Dad comes home with a BB gun for Junior.

Mom: "Dear, you know I don't approve of those things."
Dad: "It's just a BB gun."
Mom: "He's too young."
Dad: "I had one when I was his age."
Mom: "He'll hurt himself or somebody else."
Dad: "Naw, I'll teach him how to use it properly, and I'll take it away if he can't handle it."

Without a male, the boy hears only one voice. And it probably won't be the voice that takes him towards manhood, only the voice that wants to restrain his "mannish" urges.

THE DIFFICULT JOB OF A DISTANT DAD

The distance may be across town or across the country, but the important touch points remain the same.

Most distant fathers have deep and usually unstated fears. They fear that their children will blame them, hate them, or want nothing to do with them, regardless of the events that brought about the break in relationship with the birth mother. They often fear that a new male in their son's life will replace them. These fears are usually unfounded, but by believing these lies, many men end up with self-fulfilling prophecies. It doesn't need to be this way.

A blended family often complicates a dad's ability to connect with his son from a prior relationship. This is where some solid counseling can help both father and son understand that despite distance and new relationships, the boy will still be important to his dad, even if Dad is getting married again.

BOYS ARE BUILT TO IDOLIZE THEIR FATHERS.

This is a signpost of hope for distant dads.

In the dark father-son drama *Road to Perdition,* the father (Tom Hanks) is a Depression-era hit man who goes about his business and returns home like a typical, but distant, family man. Eventually, his eldest son discovers what it is that his father does for a living, thus setting up the story line of the film. In the final frames, the boy, who also narrates the movie, tries to philosophize whether his father was a good man (he provided for his family, was honorable among thieves, and served as protector for his family) or a bad man (he killed for a living). The boy ends up at the only conclusion left to him: "He was Dad." [11]

Boys do want to idolize their fathers, but it's much easier if their fathers, with or without custody of the children, give them something worth idolizing.

In order to love his father and honor him, a boy has to know him as a father.

This is where the need for keeping a connection comes in. It's a connection that boys naturally want to have but that dads must take the initiative to keep alive.

Here are a few ideas you can use to strengthen that connection.

Use the phone.

The one vital thing a distant father must do is stay in touch regularly and consistently. Brief phone calls just to say, "I'm thinking of you" mean more than you'll know to a boy, even if he doesn't appear to be interested. Don't expect that your son will reveal his world to you

[11] *Road to Perdition,* copyright © 2002 by Dream Works Pictures.

over the telephone. Sometimes the TV program or the kids calling him out to play will distract him. This is not rejection.

Send cards and notes.
Buy a stack of goofy postcards and send one off whenever you get a few spare minutes. You don't have to write a long message; just letting your child know that you're thinking of him is what matters.

E-mail your kids.
E-mail is a great way for men to stay in touch with their kids in a quick, personal way. Help your child become computer literate and keep in constant touch at the same time. You can chat in real time or, if separated by time zones, by standard E-mail.

Build memories.
Take father-son photos and send them to your son. Make sure that photos of your son occupy a place of honor in your home. You might even want to use your son's photo as a screen saver on your computer. These small things are a great way to help bind a relationship.

Building a father-son tradition is a great touch point during those times when a distant dad is able to spend time with his son. A routine, a particular restaurant, or an activity (one dad I know finds a place to skip rocks with his son during each visit) becomes the cement of memory and identification. As boys get older, the tradition may need to be replaced with a new tradition.

Celebrate the family name.
The boy most likely carries the name of the father. This is a boy's badge of identity; a wise dad can use it as a way to bond with his son. Present your son with a family crest (if you don't have one, ask an artist friend to create one for you) or prepare a family tree. Talk about family heroes and scoundrels. Help him understand that he can choose to honor or dishonor the family name. (For example, who wants to have the last name Hitler after what Adolf did to his family's honor?)

Provide a masculine environment.

Create a masculine environment where your son can see firsthand how a man is expected to respond. Anything counts here—from a game of racquetball to taking him on the road for a business trip. It all contributes to building that connection, that road toward manhood.

Make school your business.

Know the names of your son's teachers, and make sure his teachers know who you are. This helps your son know how important it is for you to be involved in his life, even from a distance.

Discipline creatively.

It's easy for the discipline process to break down in a fatherless home. As boys become teens, they often become surly and uncontrollable. A distraught ex-spouse on the phone imploring a distant dad to "do something with this kid!" is a cry coming too late. Distant dads *can* help shape the morality of their boys, but it often takes creativity, imagination, and working behind the scenes.

Naturally, the best solution is to work together with the boy's mother. This prevents a boy from playing one against the other. Where this is not possible, you'll have to invent and try other methods of distant discipline.

One dad I know, fearing his son would be sucked into the world of drugs when he hit the teen years, made a deal with his son when he was still in middle school. The father took his son to a car dealership to look at new cars. He gave his son a price and told the boy to pick out any new car in that price range. Then he made a deal with his son: If the boy stayed drug free until he graduated from high school, they would visit the car dealership again, and this time the boy could drive off in the car he had chosen.

This dad understood that the smell of new leather and the gleam of chrome and metal would create a memory for his young boy. He also knew that he was giving his son a good reason, one that would be understood by his peers, for "excusing" himself from using drugs.

This dad, who would never have bought himself a new car, told me, "It's worth twenty-five grand to me to have my boy stay away from drugs."

Granted, rewards may not be the *best* way to shape the morality or behavior of a boy, but as this father pointed out, distant dads are not often given the option of the best way. At least he was trying *something.*

Enlist the help of a spiritual mentor.

If the boy is going to a church, get together with the youth workers—particularly the male youth workers—to ask their help in mentoring the boy.

Even if your son's mother is not involved in a Christian community, make sure that your son understands the importance of your commitment to godly things. Remember, at this stage of life, the deeds and values of a man usually have far more weight than those of a woman.

Look for the unusual.

Sometimes you have to get creative. Reconsider the need to be a Disneyland Dad, with whom each weekend involves amusement and pizza.

A boy might have a far more powerful experience if you go with him on a weeklong missions trip to Haiti rather than a week's vacation to the lake.

TIPS FOR SINGLE MOTHERS

The son of a single mother is at great risk. Most studies suggest that such a boy is far more likely to be incarcerated than a boy from an intact, two-parent home—up to twice as likely. This statistic changes little even if a stepfather comes into the picture.[12]

The son of a single mom is always man hungry. He usually has no

[12] L. Alan Srouge and Susan L. Pierce, *Men in the Family: Associations with Juvenile Conduct—1999,* Washington State Dept. of Health Fact Sheet.

model upon which to base his future actions other than what he sees in the media or on the streets. It's not unusual for him to come home to an empty house or an exhausted mom.

MOMS CAN HELP THEIR SONS IN PRACTICAL WAYS.

In spite of this, there *are* practical and workable things a single mom can do to help her male children become Christian men. But it takes determination and work on her part. Here are a few tips.

Find a mentor and model.

Single women can help their sons tremendously by finding men who will act as mentors. Note: This is not husband shopping. It's completely apart from any emotional need for companionship that the mother may feel in her own life.

The best place to shop for a mentor is in the church, and the best mentors are men from stable families who already have boys of their own.

It would be wonderful if there were a ministry that naturally matched up needy boys with available male mentors. But this is not usually the case within the church. It will fall upon the mother to take a proactive role.

I would be remiss not to point out that the vulnerability factors of a needy boy and an anxious mother can be signals quickly picked up on by the predators in the world. Be very cautious and vigilant in these areas, but don't let that fear create paralysis.

Find something nice to say about his father.

Even if he turned out to be a complete creep, there had to be something about the guy that first attracted you to him. Find that one thing—his goofy sense of humor, his personal hygiene, his loyalty to friends—any sliver of positive virtue—and hold that up to the boy.

As he proceeds into manhood, your son will want to mirror his father at least in some way. It's far easier for a woman to cut off her emotional relationship with a man than it is for a boy to cut off his emotional connection to his father, even if the father is absent. For a boy, his father is part of his identity, the person to whom he looks for his imprint.

The risk, of course, is that the boy will want to seek out his birth father and emulate him, even if the man is living in dissipation. I do believe that this risk is very low. Most boys are smart enough to see the difference between a real man and the shadow of one, as disappointing as that realization may be. And most boys don't wish to emulate a shadow.

Absolutely avoid associating the boy with his father negatively. Don't say things like "That's the way your father always looked at me before he hit me," or "You're lazy, just like your father." This does no good in motivating the child towards the positive but instead builds walls between the emerging man looking for a father image and the mother who must raise him.

Do not drug your son.

For centuries, boys have run across the landscape at warp speed, fidgeted in class, and chased after mischief and adventure. Only recently have we decided to find these wild boys and drug them into submission. We poison them in order to make it easier on us.

Numerous sources indicate that currently about four million kids are being drugged into submission. The vast majority of them are boys. Consider this chilling excerpt from a recent article in the *The Massachusetts News:*

> Boys are diagnosed as having Attention Deficit Disorder far more frequently than girls. According to the Diagnostic and Statistical Manual, conduct disorder is "much more common in males." The Manual also says that ADD occurs in boys four to nine times more frequently than in girls. Michael Gurian, a family therapist and the author of five books on male develop-

ment, blames the Ritalin/ADD problem partly on absent dads and working moms. Ritalin can make things worse, he said.[13]

Before we change our kids' chemistry, we should change the way they learn and their environment. Are there children who have clinical conditions that demand some medical intervention? Yes, but precious few.

I pity the Tom Sawyers and Huck Finns of today. They're forced to gobble Ritalin and visit child psychologists because being a boisterous boy doesn't jell with our current cultural norms.

Hold on to moral authority.

This should go without saying, but I'm astonished at the number of people, even in the Christian community, who want to raise children with a standard that they themselves don't keep.

If you want your kids to stay sexually pure, *you* must stay sexually pure. If you want your son to use decent language, *you* must use decent language. The same goes for drugs, alcohol, cheating, and lying.

You can never require your son to do as you say, not as you do. What you do says what you believe and who you are. This generation is looking for authenticity and detects hypocrisy in a microsecond!

Introduce your son to man stories.

Boys love to discover heroic men. When your boys are young, read them Bible stories of great heroes of the faith—stories of adventure, conflict, and drama with the likes of David, Moses, and Joseph.

As they get older, introduce them to a wider range of godly or honorable men through books, articles, and movies. You probably won't have to force your son to drink up information about dynamic and heroic men. The thirst is already there.

[13] "'Attention Deficit Disorder' . . . Is It Real?" *The Massachusetts News*, 28 January 2002.

Don't neglect discipline.

It becomes a bit intimidating when a seventeen-year-old boy outweighs his mom by sixty pounds and stands a foot taller. How do you tell this monster he has to be in by 11:00 P.M.?

What will you do if he laughs you off?

The collapse of discipline is one of the most destructive areas in single-mother homes. Without the ability to physically intimidate a boy, many mothers give up, saying, "What can I do? I can't control him."

Actually, a mom can do a lot more than she thinks.

For one, you can take away his driving privileges. Not just the keys, but the license as well. (For many boys, their ability to drive is more important than having a left arm.)

I didn't get a driver's license until I was eighteen. The issue was hair. As a high school student in the late sixties, I wanted lots of hair; Mom wanted none of it.

It seems silly now, but it wasn't then.

Since Dad wasn't around to settle the argument and my mom figured that the hair issue was a hill she was willing to die on, she used the only power she had. She refused to sign for my license. I wanted to look cool . . . so I walked and rode my bike, looking cool.

Now you might say she *lost* that battle. Yes, she did. And perhaps it was the wrong battle to fight, but the effect it had was that it showed me that my mom was willing to use all the power she could lay her hands on to discipline me. It scared me to think what she might conjure up if I did something *really* bad. Visions of military school danced in my head.

I disliked the place where we met to do battle, but I respected her efforts. And I told her so years later.

Moms need to use tough love. They can call in male relatives as resources. But most of all, a mom can begin to build the foundation of respect early in the process of child rearing.

Any parent who has been lax in discipline during the formative years will find it very difficult to exert that control once the child reaches the teen years.

Children weren't designed by God to be raised by a single parent. But the fact is that this will be the destiny of many. We must do all we can to see to it that these children will still benefit from a loving parent that is doing his or her best—with the help of God and man.

In life, as in a football game, the principle to follow is: hit the line hard.

–Teddy Roosevelt

9 INITIATION

Deep in the north Brazilian Amazon region, a group of tribal boys squat on their haunches in the blazing sun. As they wait with sullen nervousness, they have no idea what to expect once their names are called. They only know that they will be taken one by one into the jungle to become men. Other than that, everything is draped in mystery.

When a lad's name is barked out, the nearly naked boy obediently trots into the dense greenery and disappears from view. With him are the men of the tribe, and the experience that's in store for him is both horrific and essential. To fail the experience is to be destined to be treated as a child and a weakling for the rest of his life.

Once in the jungle, the boys are instructed to locate the hole of an extremely large and savage ant called by natives the "twenty-four ant" because its wasplike sting endures for twenty-four hours. The boy builds fires around the entrance to the ant colony and ingeniously directs the smoke, funneling it into the ant hole. The heavy smoke renders the ants fairly passive for a short while. As each staggering ant is plucked from the earth, the boy quickly weaves it into a palm mat until there are sixty or seventy ants pinched between the layers of jungle fabric. The ant's head protrudes from one side of the mat, and the tail—or "business end"—from the other. In time, the drug effect of the smoke will wear off and the ants will not only be alert, they'll be furious!

Each boy is stripped of his remaining clothes and instructed to stand spread eagle. The men of the tribe then swat the stinging end of the quivering, ant-filled mat against the boy's naked body. To become a man, the boy must endure this incredible pain without a moan or whimper.

Missionaries who have witnessed this initiation rite report that on occasion the pain is so severe the boy simply passes out and collapses onto the jungle floor.

After the healing, the boys are welcomed and treated as men by the entire tribe.

The primitive world has historically created shocking rites of passage for its young men. Some of these situations are so dangerous or difficult that the possibility of death for the initiate is very real.

For many years, the entrance to manhood that included the right to get married in the African Masai tribe was based on a solo lion hunt. The inductee was given a long spear and instructions for impaling a charging lion, and then he was sent into the bush. In the case of success, the young man would return with the ears of the lion. In the case of failure, the young man would simply not return.

Knocking out a tooth or mutilating a part of the body, as practiced by the Kurnai tribe in Australia, is a variation on the common "pain and change" formula found in many rites of passage.

Passage into manhood in many of these tribal cultures is definitive and costly. An inductee knows when and where he has crossed the line into manhood. In many cases, he has been altered physically as confirmation of that passage.

Interestingly, inner-city gangs, the military, and—until it became politically incorrect and in some cases, illegal—even college fraternities often use some form of initiation rite as a ticket to their inner circle. Some of these initiations echo strongly with the kinds of things done in uncivilized realms.

Often those of us who live in "modern times" presume that we have nothing to learn from the past or the primitive. We shake our heads in enlightened arrogance at the barbarism of these tribal rites and dismiss their relevance out of hand.

But perhaps in our rush to embrace whatever is new and to divorce ourselves from our past, we have chucked overboard some important lessons in the way that values are transferred in our communities.

It's quite possible that we have much more to learn from slower, ancient societies than we think. Especially if we get past the sometimes-distasteful external actions practiced by some cultures and take a look at the important elements, ideas, and principles behind their initiations.

Boys in western cultures have stumbled into manhood for decades, and the concept of having a defining moment that assures manhood could be exactly what today's boy needs.

Let me be very clear here. God's value for the sanctity of life teaches us that a Christian rite of passage doesn't have to be gory or excruciating in order to be valid. It does, however, have to be meaningful.

Just as the ability to withstand severe physical pain is real and meaningful in the context of the jungle, modern men must display abilities that are just as real and demanding.

An initiation is important to a man because it is an act of identification by those other males whose esteem is important. Boys seek out that esteem and will often act out in unnecessarily dangerous ways to get it.

Ironically, this passing into manhood doesn't seem to have as much to do with the boy's personal bravery as it does with that bravery being identified and celebrated. For many young men, the recognition of their importance as a man can actually bring out attributes and abilities that might have otherwise lain dormant.

William Wellman was a pugnacious, rough, brawling little adventurer who joined up with the French air force during World War I and had already seen action by the time America joined the war.

Wounded after a terrible crash, Wellman came back to the United States, where fighting aviators were considered the toast of the town. Finding his way to California, "Wild Bill Wellman" rubbed shoulders with the movie celebrities of the day and soon found work on the Hollywood film lot of Samuel Goldwyn.

Unfortunately, a job on the movie lot was no guarantee of a career in front of or behind the camera. The young Wellman became a low-level gofer and was quickly forgotten by his celebrity pals in the movie business.

One day Goldwyn announced that the studio was to have a special visitor. The famous head of the U.S. army, General John J. Pershing, would be coming for a tour the following day. Goldwyn, in an effort to show just how patriotic his company employees were, asked every man who had served in the armed forces to don his old uniform when he reported to work the next day.

When Pershing arrived, he was greeted by hundreds of men in army green uniforms standing stiffly at attention. Among the men was Bill Wellman. He was wearing the sky blue uniform of Lafayette Escadrille, the French-American flying forces. Across his chest were the medals he had received for bravery. The unique uniform and medals caught the general's eye. He, unlike the studio personnel, knew their merit. Pershing approached Wellman and drew near to shake his hand. As the old general clasped the young man's hand, he said, "Son, let me know if there is anything I can do for you." Wellman drew a bit closer to the general and in a quiet voice he said, "Sir, there is one thing you could do for me. You could act as if I were somebody important."

And the old warhorse did just that. He made a big deal out of William Wellman. Such a big deal that "Wild Bill Wellman" suddenly found himself in front of *and* behind a camera. In the end, he felt more comfortable behind the camera as a director.

Wellman went on to direct dozens of films in a career that spanned four decades. His works included *The Oxbow Incident, Beau Geste, A Star Is Born,* and the first film ever to be rewarded with an Oscar—the World War I aviation adventure, *Wings.*

Wellman's potential was realized when his bravery was recognized by the men to whom he needed it to matter. Indeed, men who have been accepted into a group of men often find themselves pushed beyond their natural boundaries to performances they never realized that they could do.

Of course, Bill Wellman was a man far before he was commended by the general and would have been a man even if the general had passed him by without comment.

Whenever manhood is bestowed upon a boy, it's because men are "acting or pretending" that the boy is somebody important. Men are honoring him not for a life that *has been* lived well, but for a life that *will be,* with God's help, lived well. Men see and affirm the potential in the boy to become a man.

Samuel did very much the same with the young David as Pershing did with Wellman. David was seen by his family as an insignificant specimen of manhood, yet he was God's one and only choice for the future King of Israel.

But for a considerable time after his anointing, the "king" of Israel spent his long, tedious days governing sheep (see 1 Samuel 16).

All initiation processes are similar in that those who matter in the lives of young men are the ones who must give them the recognition they are seeking. Whether the man lives out his manhood to its fullest potential or lives in perpetual adolescence depends greatly upon being settled and assured of his place in the world of men.

By looking at the common threads in both past and present initiation rites, we can see patterns that lead to a meaningful entry into manhood.

Although these patterns are somewhat distasteful if followed in the primitive fashion, they still offer important insight into the world of men. By studying these patterns, we can craft this information into consequential, God honoring, and acceptable induction ceremonies or modern rites of passage to use with our own boys.

Note how these patterns have parallels in the church. In Christ we find our significance, meaning, and worth . . . just as every man and wanna-be man must. In addition to having a personal relationship with our Savior, we must become part of a church community and be embraced by it. We enter the church via initiation rituals: baptism, Communion, confirmation, or membership. We affirm the standards of the Christian community and take upon ourselves the responsibilities of that community.

And there's always the possibility of failure. If we deny the essentials of the faith, we will not be counted as part of the Christian community. Some churches also use excommunication as a way to set a spiritual troublemaker outside the circle of the church.

With that in mind, let's take a look at some common essentials found in initiation rites throughout the world.

The process is individual. Becoming a man is something that occurs away from the main and mixed group. It's a personal and private act, not a team achievement. The community provides the resources, but the individual must choose to use them in order to become mature. "We" do not become men. "I" become a man.

Rugged individualism is something Americans intuitively understand. It's an honored part of our culture and is celebrated in countless films and books. The idea that being a true man often means standing alone is usually built into the initiation process.

The only "we" in the initiation rite is found in the community of men. The community tests the individual so that when he is alone he can still be a man.

The process is not comfortable. Ancient cultures understood that the role of a man often called for sacrifice, danger, and the possibility of pain. Some kind of discomfort or pain is often part of initiation rites. This not only appeals to the male idea of *macho* but also is used to psychologically prepare the initiate for the possibility of discomfort as he takes on the role of a man in his society.

The process is male initiated. Women can't lead men into manhood. It's an exclusive club. Men generally care far more about what other men think of them than they do about what women think of them. Boys in particular are looking for the affirmation of men. They may accept the affection and pleasure of girls, but they know that their manhood does not come from them. In fact, women usually have nothing to do with male initiation rites. In many cultures, interaction with women in a mature sense can only begin after successful completion of the rite of passage. Males bring other males into manhood. Males set the standard to be met, supervise the initiate, and acknowledge his success or failure in achieving manhood.

Men are keepers of the "code" that it takes to be a man. The initiate can only learn the code from other men.

The process is mysterious. Initiation rites are often kept secret from the larger culture. This mystery sets the initiates apart and creates an aura of power and wonder in those yet uninitiated.

In addition, most initiation rites are held in locations away from everyday life activities. The removal of all things familiar puts the initiate to the test as an individual alone in a potentially hostile world.

The process requires courage. Males live in a world dominated by the need to demonstrate courage. A man knows that in the event of crisis, disaster, or even catching and killing the mouse in the house, *he,* not the women or children, will be called to action. Virtually all initiation rites require an element of courage. While the kind of courage that modern men are called to may be somewhat different from ancient times, men still understand that they must be brave.

The process requires separation. All initiation rites have a universal ingredient of separating the initiate from the company of boys, girls, and women—particularly their mothers. In some cultures this is a long and arduous process during which the boy is actually considered dead by his mother. In other cultures, the boy is actually snatched (sometimes with the quiet collusion of the mother) from his boyish routine to begin the process of becoming a man.

Other than support, the role of women in the initiation process is generally zero. Women are almost never allowed to participate, and very often the actual initiation process is kept secret from women.

This separation is not done because women are of a lesser class but because the role of husband, provider, and protector can only be demonstrated to boys by men.

The process produces change. A common element in many initiation rites is some kind of change on the part of the initiate. Typically this is a physical change such as mutilating the body or cutting the hair, but it can also be a relocation of the boy to another place within the village after initiation. Sometimes the rite will involve symbolism such as new ornamentation or the privilege to wear the sign or clothing of a man. The rite of passage changes the responsibilities of the new young "man" and allows for greater interaction and acceptance between the men of the tribe and the inductee. It signals an end to childhood and the start of a new kind of life.

In some cultures, this change is typified by a death ritual wherein the initiate undergoes a mock death and rebirth—a device echoed in the main Christian initiation rite, baptism.

Any kind of initiation rite without some kind of genuine change in the status and role of an inductee would lose its significance.

The process ends with celebration and acceptance. The end of the initiation process is commonly celebrated not only by the men of the community but also by the community as a whole. The inductees have left as boys and returned as men who are now ready to serve in that capacity.

A community celebration is the crowning point of any initiation event. In this way, both the initiate and the community gather together to affirm the values they subscribe to and rejoice in the fact that there is another generation prepared to carry on those ideas and values.

CHRISTIAN INITIATION

The early church was deeply rooted in Judaic practices. The entry of boys into the family of men was couched in a deeply spiritual context. A sample of this can be found in the only account we have of Jesus' youth:

> Every year his parents went to Jerusalem for the Feast of the Passover. When he was twelve years old, they went up to the Feast, according to the custom. After the Feast was over, while his parents were returning home, the boy Jesus stayed behind in Jerusalem, but they were unaware of it. Thinking he was in their company, they traveled on for a day. Then they began looking for him among their relatives and friends. When they did not find him, they went back to Jerusalem to look for him. After three days they found him in the temple courts, sitting among the teachers, listening to them and asking them questions. Everyone who heard him was amazed at his understanding and his answers. When his parents saw him, they were astonished. His mother said to him, "Son, why have you treated us like this? Your father and I have been anxiously searching for you."
>
> "Why were you searching for me?" he asked. "Didn't you know I had to be in my Father's house?" But they did not understand what he was saying to them. (Luke 2:41-50)

Since the practice of the ancient temple was to segregate men from women and children (as well as foreigners), something significant had to occur before a boy could cross the threshold into the temple court area and have dialogue with the men there. That something is what is now referred to as the bar mitzvah, a rite of passage for those moving into an age of accountability. The implication is that at this Feast of the Passover, Jesus went through a ceremony that enabled him to enter the court of men.

While the early church appears not to have continued the bar mitzvah practice, they had no shortage of initiation rites.

Baptism is clearly a rite of passage not only from childhood to adulthood but from one citizenship to another—from rebellion to faithful child, from serving sin to serving righteousness.

In another important way, Christian baptism mirrors a common thread in most pagan rites of passage: a passage from death to new life (the principle of *change*). The initiate renounces his life as a child, dies to it, and is reborn as an adult. The Christian renounces his life of sin and is reborn as a child of God.

The ancient Latin word for these rites of the church is *sacramentum.* The word has military roots; it was the same name used for the oath a soldier took when joining the Roman army. It was a promise to forsake the comforts of civilian life and to serve, wholly and sacrificially, the cause of the emperor and Rome. The early church fathers saw that becoming a Christian was similar to joining the military in that it took a strong, courageous, and sacrificial decision to live as a believer.

So tough were these new Christian rites in their implication that the early church had no trouble recruiting men into their ranks. The initiation into the faith was, at times, by virtue of its extreme danger and cost, an initiation into genuine manhood or womanhood.

Sadly, Christianity is often not seen as a desirable choice for an aggressive, strong male. This does not mean that the elements men of ancient times saw and identified with are any less meaningful today. It may, however, indicate that we haven't done a very good job of communicating those strengths in a way that men can relate to.

It may be difficult to convince adult men of the masculine vitality inherent in following the God of the Bible, but it's certainly not too late to communicate to those boys still groping for genuine manhood.

The New Age movement and some racial groups have, in the last decade, already sensed the vacuum and raced to fill it— often with bizarre and laughable results, such as "dream circles" connecting with the "inner self through drumming, toning, and vision casting," or by appealing to pagan Celtic or tribal African rituals.

I believe it's the Christian church that holds the real solution.

Perhaps it's time to introduce a new rite into what we celebrate in our community of faith—a rite that contains elements, possibly even primitive ones, that men quickly identify with and yet are honoring to Christ, relevant to the pressures of being a man in today's world, and doable for the typical church. (This does not include being beaten with an ant mat.)

For an initiation rite to be powerful, meaningful, and life changing, each of the attributes listed above should be carefully crafted into an experience that each boy is called to enter into.

The elements you choose to include in a rite of passage should resonate with the teachings of Scripture and with the obvious and God-designed temperament of the boys and men in your church. Thus equipped, you can reclaim a milestone that once was as prevalent as the other rituals by which we mark important moments and choices in life: marriage, baptism, graduations, and even funerals.

A rite of passage is not a step backward to the primitive; it's a cultural imperative that has been neglected in our rush to embrace modern lifestyle—a lifestyle that has created lost boys, spiritually bankrupt men, and a society adrift on dangerous seas.

And the more I considered Christianity, the more I found that while it had established a rule and order, the chief aim of that order was to give room for good things to run wild.

–G. K. Chesterton
Orthodoxy

10 WHAT THE CHURCH MUST DO

I am a churchman.

I believe the church is the primary device that God has ordained to take the message of his love and hope to the world.

While I appreciate the wonderful work that has been done by the wide range of parachurch organizations that seem to continually sprout up, I believe most are only in existence because we in the church have failed to catch God's vision, sense his imagination, or had the guts to roll up our sleeves and do the hard, challenging, and sacrificial work we've been called to do. The church should be working in the streets; the church should be on the cutting edge of creativity and excellence; the church should be patron of the arts; the church should be a bastion of intellectual prowess and a refuge for the broken. We need to be the champions of those lost in the shuffle, the primary spreaders of the "good infection" of the gospel, and beacons of hope and guidance to our culture.

I've chosen to throw my lot in with the church. And at times, the church has been the most difficult place to work and serve.

Just like the rest of the world, the local church is often myopic, fearful, petty, cheap, backbiting, alternately bureaucratic and dictatorial, and ridiculously slow to alter its ways. The church says it wants to reach the lost, but when the lost do appear on its doorsteps in their gritty, unwashed, and untamed state, the church becomes full of fear and loathing and demands that these people change instantly or be gone. The modern church wants to see salvation and growth on its own terms.

Yet I believe it should be, can be, and hopefully will be the church that makes the difference in how men and boys perceive and welcome the message of Christ. I believe it is the church that has the greatest power to reach, welcome, and keep boys as they make the journey into manhood.

It would be folly to think that all of Christendom will suddenly awake to the fact that men are sorely underrepresented in our communities. It would be even greater folly to believe that all who come to that realization will be willing to take the tough steps necessary to reverse the trend. But if churches, one by one, here and there, start to rethink how they relate the truths of God to men and boys and begin to take action, we'll soon see a significant difference.

Change has never been popular within the church. Change threatens the status quo. People fear that change will open the door to theological compromise or loss of historical distinction. Change often offends, causes us to lose members, and affects our bottom line. But for the church to draw men in, attract and keep boys into maturity, and bequeath the gift of manhood, it needs to change.

This change should not be one that creates some kind of old-boy network or jock club. It should not exclude women or put them on the sidelines. It does, however, involve learning to speak the native tongue of the male species.

The change that we need to make comes in two varieties: those things that will make the church inviting to men and those things that will attract, affirm, and hold on to boys as they grow into manhood.

How do we do this? Let's look at some necessary first steps.

BECOME A RISKY, GUTSY CHURCH

The greatest way to attract men won't be found in programs but in a church that dares to live by the teachings of Jesus Christ. This kind of church requires men to take seriously the fact that their citizenship is not of this earth. It requires that men honestly believe that the best way to be a great man is to make other people feel great. It requires that men become more concerned about spiritual satisfaction than about accumulation of possessions. It requires men to rethink the presumptions of our culture and live different, daring, and radical lives.

FIND MORE MALE TEACHERS

Finding male teachers, particularly for students in fourth grade and up, is imperative. We must separate the classes and groups into boys and girls, regardless of the size, and a male teacher needs to handle the boys. This is key to growth.

In the typical church, the role of teaching is usually left to women. If we want to encourage male volunteers, we need to offer some education, motivation, and recruitment in order to get men to fill these roles.

Christian teaching methods must also be redefined so that males feel empowered to teach in ways that express their masculinity.

DEVELOP MINISTRIES ORIENTED TOWARD YOUNG ALPHA MALES

Those in charge of children's groups must revisit their timetables, teaching materials, and learning environments, in light of what it takes to grab and hold the strongest males in the group. This doesn't mean we have to give up teaching; it does mean we might have to teach in a completely different manner.

In addition, ministries with a strong male emphasis should be encouraged and developed outside the regular church gathering times.

These ministries might require the church to make some unusual investments. For example, as part of our strategy to draw young males, our church is building a skateboard park on our property. Paintball guns, climbing walls, rappelling gear, even a go-cart track or BMX track (for those with property to spare) may join the standard fare of basketball hoops and volleyball nets. Indoors, the youth room might have a wall dedicated to a bank of TV screens and a load of Playstations.

The common thread of all these activities and investments is that they are guy oriented. Girls may participate to some degree, but the target audience for these things is primarily male.

This is not to imply an either/or kind of focus. It would be wonderful if, simultaneous to what I'm suggesting for the boys, the church would encourage a "chicks who rip" movement. The idea is to work for excellence with both genders. But if one has to err, better to err by leaning toward guys.

PITCH TOWARD MEN

Marketing experts know how to target an audience. They work hard to create a certain impression and their ads and commercials are carefully crafted to target the gender and demographics of their potential customers.

The Christian church often pretends that it does not have to enter the marketplace of ideas. We think people will somehow find out about us and somehow drift into our chairs.

Consider what would happen if we decided to take our publicity money and efforts and gear them toward men.

For just one example of how this might play out, let's look at how the typical church advertises itself. Many churches put ads in the religion section of the local newspaper. This section typically comes out once a week and is considered a graveyard section. Men generally flip past this section as fast as they do the food and recipe sections that show up midweek.

If we were creating an ad to connect with men, the first thing we'd need to do is to move it to the sports page. Yep, right there with the ads for adult nightclubs, bars, and auto-body repair.

Not only that, but the ad would have to appeal to a man's masculine sensibilities. Flowery script and warm, fuzzy imagery wouldn't work. The ad would have to be strong, bold, and compelling to males.

AVOID PUTTING WOMEN IN LEADERSHIP OVER MEN

We live in a world that has, in most areas, accommodated itself to the egalitarian idea of equal opportunity for the sexes. No matter how most men might feel about a woman in authority in the workplace or as a doctor or dentist, there are places where men bristle at the idea of a woman in leadership.

One such area is the military, particularly in combat sections. Professional male sports are another area where resistance to women in leadership is high.

For a long time, the church was also on this list. But today, a woman at the helm is becoming more and more acceptable, particularly in mainline Protestant denominations and in some Pentecostal groups.

This is not to say that women are incapable of the godly wisdom and insight it takes to shepherd a flock. But it's true that men, particularly strong males, are resistant to female leadership in the spiritual realm.

From time to time, God does put a woman in a leadership role. The Old Testament records that Deborah became a judge, a leader of Israel. The book of Acts tells us clearly that Priscilla had a coleadership role with her husband in the early church. God has used women in the present and past as leaders and visionaries. Mother Teresa inspired men *and* women by her leadership right up to her death of old age in 1997.

But women in leadership roles are the exception, not the rule. Typically, men are uncomfortable with the idea of sitting under a woman as a senior pastor or in any other position of authority.

Now, we could wage a theological argument over the appropriateness of women in church leadership if we wanted to. The model of our Lord with his twelve often bumbling but singularly male staff members trailing behind him may give us a clue. In addition, the teachings and practices of the New Testament church as seen in the pages of Scripture seem tilted toward male leadership in the role of overseer or pastor.

We could add to the argument the weight of thousands of years of Christian practice and teaching. The historic Christian church has been virtually unanimous on the understanding that male leadership of the church was designed and intended by God—an idea that was not seriously challenged until recent times. But regardless of where a person ends up on the issue, the solution may be more than biblical; it's pragmatic: *Even if you can, it doesn't always mean you should.*

Are men who are uncomfortable with women leading them in ministry roles merely brutes, blinded by years of prejudice, who need to open their spiritual eyes, or are they responding to something deeper—an "order of things" that's part of the divine stamp? I would argue the latter. I would argue that within a context, men are born to lead and women are born to follow. Scripture seems to echo this structure (see 1 Corinthians 11:3). I even think that most women would agree.

Even a weak male in leadership is less distasteful to most men than a woman in leadership.

Strong males in leadership are magnetic for both men and women.

DEVELOP MALE-ORIENTED YOUTH GROUPS

Strong males should be the common denominator for the things that go on in youth groups. Most youth groups are girl heavy. Many youth workers don't know how to attract strong males to their church activities. In addition, girls are often more verbal about spiritual things, tend to value relationship building, and are quicker to take on roles of leadership within the group. In short, girls are somewhat easier to work with because they're usually more cooperative and respond better than boys.

But a female-driven youth group eventually leads to a female-driven church. Youth leaders must aggressively seek out strong males and draw them into leadership within the group.

There's an old rule of thumb in youth ministry that says, "Go after the guys and you'll get the girls; go after the girls and you'll get only guys who are after your girls."

The rationale is simple: Once you have a roomful of guys—particularly strong, masculine guys—the girls will show up as well. It doesn't work so well the other way around. The hobby of guys is generally not girls; it's some kind of sport or other endeavor.

Going after boys should be the serious business of any youth leader. Any less than a fifty-fifty boy-girl ratio in a youth group is a call for alarm. Not that we should ignore the girls. A rip-roaring girls' ministry ought to be paired with a rip-roaring boys' ministry. But since the boys are harder to reach, we often need to put forth extra energy and focus in that area.

Successfully reaching boys is easier when we concentrate on the younger teens, particularly those in middle school. Boys at this age run in packs. Each pack has its own personality, pecking order, and interest level. All a youth leader needs to do is to figure out what will motivate a given group of kids (skateboarding, motor cross, paintball, surfing, hunting, basketball, music, etc.) and tap into that vein in a creative way.

ENCOURAGE MAN-TO-MAN ACCOUNTABILITY

Men are funny creatures. In mixed company, we rarely let our guard down. Some instinct kicks in that makes us think we need to at least "play the man" if women are around. Even in a larger company of men, we may choose to stand aloof, cross our arms in distance-keeping safety, and do a lot of taking stock.

But get us with some trusted friends, and somewhere between the joking and shoptalk some deep and incredible things will happen.

I meet with a group of four other men every Wednesday evening. Each of these men comes from a far different walk of life than I do. One of the men lived as a hippie long after the hippie movement lost its flower power. All through the seventies, eighties, and nineties, he was the man that time forgot, camped out in a small shack with few amenities, growing his own "grass" as income to supply his ever-increasing habit . . . until Jesus got hold of him. We still can't get him to eat meat, though.

Another one of the guys has tattoos marking just about every inch of his body as well as numerous piercings. He starts to get nervous if a meeting goes on too long, due to his need for a cigarette (this being the last addiction he has to conquer in a long and hideous line of addictions).

A third man is a burly salesman with whitened teeth who finally in his forties found a spiritual craving that he only recently has begun to satisfy.

Our final group member came to Kauai to die but found eternal life instead. He was a longtime member of the San Francisco gay community and suffered from AIDS. His life is a battleground of emotions as he faces physical deterioration and sorts through the consequences that occur when one surrenders every part of his life, including sexual desires and actions, to the will of God.

Even though we have a common bond in Jesus, our backgrounds

and the levels of our Christian experience are vastly different. But there is a cement of accountability and a sense of safety among us. None of these men will slip unnoticed through the cracks of the church. If one of us falls prey to sin, there are a lot of arms reaching out to help pull him up.

MAKE YOUR MEN'S GROUP PRACTICAL AND MEANINGFUL

Men like to *do* things, so getting men together for mere socialization or a spiritual moment is hollow without the "doing" part. Mere relationship building or spiritual teaching is not enough for most men. They feel most invigorated when they have a chance to work out their salvation through some kind of purposeful activity.

As the book of James so eloquently explains, "Faith and works, works and faith, fit together hand in glove" (James 2:20, *The Message*). Our spirituality should work itself into some kind of action. And men love action!

One group of men I know developed relationships with each other and attracted other men into the life of the church by creating a father-daughter experience each quarter. Typically, the men would plan some kind of event that would be fun for both the men and the daughters. On occasion, it would be a larger event such as a ski weekend; other times it was simply dinner, bowling, or another local activity.

The men discussed these quarterly events with friends and workers and found other men, many from non-Christian backgrounds, anxious to join the group. The end result was that many of those men found their way to faith.

Other men's groups have taken on fund-raising projects or short-term missions projects as their point of purpose.

Men's groups that tie periodic projects into the mix of spiritual objectives are attractive to other men.

CREATE A RITE OF PASSAGE

Because boys need to know what it takes to be a man, because manhood must be bestowed and earned, and because the Christian church should be the best qualified to know what is required for godly manhood, it's important that we create the milestone and set the standard for our boys. This is best done in a formal, well thought out, intentional experience that draws upon the strength that God provides: a Christ-centered rite of passage.

This rite of passage should be created by a community of Christian men: fathers, uncles, brothers, and friends. These men should facilitate the rite with their own stock of boys in mind, and the results should be celebrated by the church as a whole.

What should this look like? How should it be run? Obviously there is no prescribed model in Scripture or in our culture. But basically, a modern-day rite of passage must be faithful to the standards of maturity outlined in the Bible, challenging and meaningful to the initiate, created and enacted by men, and celebrated by the rest of the community.

For those who may want to see a workable, transferable example, I've included a short outline of our own church's Passed Thru Fire rite of passage. I've also partnered with Standard Publishing to create resources that your church can use as part of a focused but flexible program called Passed Thru Fire.

PASSED THRU FIRE—A MODEL

The idea of a powerful, Christ-centered rite of passage provided by a local Christian community is not mere theory. It's an event that is actually being done by some churches.

Our church, Kauai Christian Fellowship, has created a wildly successful weekend event—Passed Thru Fire—that can be used as a template regardless of your location across the country.

The following ideas, taken from our event, aren't meant to be a rigid formula, but rather concepts to consider as you craft your own meaningful rite of passage experience. You'll need to customize these ideas to the personality and sensibilities of your own local community of faith.

Some will enjoy the brevity of this section and use the ideas as a springboard for their own imagination. Others may wish for a more structured and detailed resource. For that, I'd recommend exploring my companion *Passed Thru Fire* event package produced by Standard Publishing that gives churches the resources to create events that turn boys into men.

- **TAKE A WEEKEND.** Initiation should be a process. A one-day or afternoon event probably won't do justice to the enormity of this milestone.

- **PREPARE YOUR MEN.** Many men in the church will not have done much thinking about a rite of passage for young teens. It's important to sell the idea before embarking on creating the event. This is generally very easy, and men seem to resonate quickly with the concept.

- **CHOOSE YOUR LOCATION WISELY.** The more rural and unfamiliar the location is to your boys, the better. A wilderness camp is ideal. The main thing is to make sure there are no distractions or other campers in the area. Look for grounds where something holy can happen.

- **FOCUS ON BOYS IN GRADES SEVEN THROUGH NINE.** During the first few years of puberty, changes are coming fast and furious. Manhood is in question and childhood is in doubt. It's an ideal time to connect with boys.

- **MAKE THE EVENT MYSTERIOUS.** The men who are participating should know what's going on; the rest of the folks, including the boys, should know as little as possible. (Our subtitle for the camp publicity said only, "Leave a boy, return a man.")

- **MAKE THE EVENT EXCLUSIVE TO MEN AND BOYS.** This should go without saying, but there should be no women involved in the event at all. (Helping behind the scenes is fine.)

- **KEEP THE BOYS SEPARATE FROM THE MEN UNTIL THEY'VE FINISHED WITH THE PASSAGE.** Make the difference between boys and men clear. Separate meal tables (men *always* eat first), separate sleeping quarters, separate bedtimes, etc. We went as far as to not allow the kids to sleep in our cabins, telling them they weren't worthy of the company of men. We tossed them some tarps and rope and told them to figure out how to stay warm and dry outside.

- **CREATE ORDEALS.** Ordeals are hurdles that the boys must cross in order to be considered men. The actual kinds of ordeals are up to you, but they should include hardship (e.g., a rugged early morning hike), discipline (e.g., make at least half the hike in silence), suffering (e.g., missing a meal in order to identify with the weak and hurting of the world), conquering fear (e.g., a ropes course), courage and solitude (e.g., surviving alone in the woods in the middle of the night, while you're watching from a distance, of course), and spiritual guidance (e.g., using a compass while learning about being led by the Holy Spirit and the "true north" of the Word). Each boy must pass through a final ordeal alone in the company of men. You may want to consider creating a way for initiates to measure the ordeals as they pass them—a painted mark, a hiking stick that's branded or notched, or a token of some kind.

  Note: Ordeals should be difficult but passable. If you have kids who are impaired in one way or another, simply change the nature of *their* ordeal or require the kind of teamwork that forces the boys to help their teammate. (Use the principle found among combat troops: "No one gets left behind.")

- **CREATE A WAY FOR MEN TO TELL THEIR STORIES.** Boys need to hear from men. If you outline in advance the attributes you wish to impress upon the boys, men will have a chance to tell stories that dovetail with the characteristics of manhood you're emphasizing.

- **HAVE A STANDARD OF MANHOOD TO AVOW.** Choose the characteristics that you think are most important for men to have (we chose courage, integrity, righteousness, self-control, love for the weak and unlovely, and loyalty) and give individuals a chance to pledge to those standards. Wherever possible, tie an ordeal to a standard. For example, we had our hungry boys eat the typical evening meal of a third world family (watery soup and a bit of rice) after a physically tiring day. This came right after a session where we talked about the fact that real men care for the suffering, the unlovely, and the hurting in the world.

- **AWARD NEW "MEN" WITH A SYMBOL THAT REPRESENTS THEIR NEW LIFE.** We used a necklace with a different bead for each attribute of a man. A ring, coat of arms, or new name can work too.

- **CELEBRATE THE PASSING.** Celebrate at the event and later in a ceremony with the whole church. Make hamburgers of the fatted calf! Celebrate and party! Recognize and rejoice with those who have "passed through fire."

- **GIVE EACH NEW MAN A WINGMAN.** A wingman is a man from the church who takes on the responsibility to keep an eye on the young man, encourage him, pray for him, meet with him, teach him, and disciple him. The wingman should work with the father of the young man, but should not be his father.

- **WELCOME THE NEW MEN INTO THE RANKS OF MEN.** After the boys have successfully completed their passage, bring them into the cabins, sit with them at meals and meetings, and help them to sense their change in status. After the event, call these young men to participate in things adult men may do in the church.

- **KEEP THE EVENT DETAILS A SECRET.** Ask the initiates not to share what goes on with younger boys. Warn them that giving away some of the hardships will allow boys to cheat or prepare for what is to come. It generally takes little to motivate those who "pass through fire" to make sure the next rank of initiates has to work as hard for the passage as they did. The mystery is part of the allure for upcoming kids.

In the end, the church must become a place where "good things run wild." We must tear down the fences we have created and take some dangerous risks. We must lead the way for our children and those children who have no fathers. We must set the standard of manhood high and require our boys to reach for it. We must become a group of bold adventurers and warriors, for it's only these kinds of men who attract other men. And it's these kinds of men that we've always wanted to be.

HELP YOUR CHURCH LEAD BOYS INTO GODLY MANHOOD . . .

THE PASSED THRU FIRE EXPERIENCE

This six-session experience for guiding boys into godly manhood is a practical tool for helping parents and youth leaders launch a meaningful, Christ-centered rite of passage for the teenage boys in their church.

The kit comes complete with the following resources:

- Sixty-minute DVD with fast-paced video clips that focus on the attributes of a godly man
- Six-session leader's guide
- Pre-event tips for parents and mentors
- Event promotional materials
- Weekend retreat schedule
- Plans for an all-church commissioning service

"We went through fire and water, but you brought us to a place of abundance."

PSALM 66:12

AVAILABLE FROM YOUR LOCAL CHRISTIAN BOOKSTORE OR STANDARD PUBLISHING.
WWW.STANDARDPUB.COM